STECK-VAUGHN

TABE®
Fundamentals

Focus on Skills

Language and Spelling

LEVEL D

2nd Edition

Steck Vaughn™

HOUGHTON MIFFLIN HARCOURT
Supplemental Publishers

www.SteckVaughn.com
800-531-5015

Photo Credits: Page iv: ©Bluestone Productions/SuperStock Royalty Free; 2,47: ©Photodisc/Getty Images Royalty Free; 4: ©Veer Royalty Free.

Illustrations: Pp. 13, 27, 52 Jim Haynes; pp. 15, 23, 25, 50, 61, 66 Andrew Lankes; pp. 11, 17, 43, 54 Francine Mastrangelo; pp. 21, 33, 35, 36, 39, 46, 59 Bob Novak.

Reviewers

Victor Gathers
> Regional Coordinator of Adult Services
> New York City Department of Education
> Brooklyn Adult Learning Center
> Brooklyn, New York

Brannon Lentz
> Assistant Director of Adult Education/Skills Training
> Northwest Shoals Community College
> Muscle Shoals, Alabama

Jean Pierre-Pipkin, Ed.D.
> Director of Beaumont I.S.D. Adult Education
> Cooperative Consortium
> Beaumont, Texas

ISBN-13: 978-1-4190-5357-3
ISBN-10:   1-4190-5357-4

© 2009, 2004 Steck-Vaughn, an imprint of HMH Supplemental Publishers Inc.

Steck-Vaughn is a trademark of HMH Supplemental Publishers Inc.

TABE® is a trademark of McGraw-Hill, Inc. Such company has neither endorsed nor authorized this publication.

Printed in the United States of America.

6 7 8 9   1689   15 14 13 12

4500340528

Contents

To the Learner

Congratulations on your decision to study for the TABE! You are taking an important step in your educational career. This book will help you do your best on the TABE. You'll also find hints and strategies that will help you prepare for test day. Practice these skills—your success lies in your hands.

What Is the TABE?

TABE stands for the Tests of Adult Basic Education. These paper-and-pencil tests, published by McGraw-Hill, measure your progress on basic skills. There are five tests in all: Reading, Mathematics Computation, Applied Mathematics, Language, and Spelling.

TABE Levels M, D, and A

Test	Number of Items	Suggested Working Time (in minutes)
1 Reading	50	50
2 Mathematics Computation	25	15
3 Applied Mathematics	50	50
4 Language	55	39
5 Spelling	20	10

Test 1 Reading

This test measures basic reading skills. The main concepts covered by this test are word meaning, critical thinking, and understanding basic information.

Many things on this test will look familiar to you. They include documents and forms necessary to your everyday life, such as directions, bank statements, maps, and consumer labels. The test also includes items that measure your ability to find and use information from a dictionary, table of contents, or library computer display. The TABE also tests a learner's understanding of fiction and nonfiction passages.

Test 2 Mathematics Computation

Test 2 covers adding, subtracting, multiplying, and dividing. On the test you must use these skills with whole numbers, fractions, decimals, integers, and percents.

The skills covered in the Mathematics Computation test are the same skills you use daily to balance your checkbook, double a recipe, or fix your car.

Test 3 | Applied Mathematics

The Applied Mathematics test links mathematical ideas to real-world situations. Many things you do every day require basic math. Making budgets, cooking, and doing your taxes all take math. The test covers pre-algebra, algebra, and geometry, too. Adults need to use all these skills.

Some questions will relate to one theme. Auto repairs could be the subject, for example. The question could focus on the repair schedule. For example, you know when you last had your car repaired. You also know how often you have to get it repaired. You might have to predict the next maintenance date.

Many of the items will not require you to use a specific strategy or formula to get the correct answer. Instead this test challenges you to use your own problem-solving strategies to answer the question.

Test 4 | Language

The Language test asks you to analyze different types of writing. Examples are business letters, resumes, job reports, and essays. For each task, you have to show you understand good writing skills.

The questions fit adult interests and concerns. Some questions ask you to think about what is wrong in the written material. In other cases, you will correct sentences and paragraphs.

Test 5 | Spelling

In everyday life, you need to spell correctly, especially in the workplace. The spelling words on this test are words that many people misspell and words that are commonly used in adult writing.

Test-Taking Tips

1. Read the directions very carefully. Make sure you read through them word for word. If you are not sure what the question says, ask the person giving the test to explain it to you.

2. Read each question carefully. Make sure you know what it means and what you have to do.

3. Read all of the answers carefully, even if you think you know the answer.

4. Make sure that the reading supports your answer. Don't answer without checking the reading. Don't rely only on outside knowledge.

5. Answer all of the questions. If you can't find the right answer, rule out the answers that you know are wrong. Then try to figure out the right answer. If you still don't know, make your best guess.

6. If you can't figure out the answer, put a light mark by the question and come back to it later. Erase your marks before you finish.

7. Don't change an answer unless you are sure your first answer is wrong. Usually your first idea is the correct answer.

8. If you get nervous, stop for a while. Take a few breaths and relax. Then start working again.

How to Use *TABE Fundamentals*

Step-by-Step Instruction In Levels M and D, each lesson starts with step-by-step instruction on a skill. The instruction contains examples and then a test example with feedback. This instruction is followed by practice questions. Work all of the questions in the lesson's practice and then check your work in the Answers and Explanations in the back of the book.

The Level A books contain practice for each skill covered on the TABE. Work all of the practice questions and then check your work in the Answers and Explanations in the back of the book.

Reviews The lessons in Levels M and D are grouped by a TABE Objective. At the end of each TABE Objective, there is a Review. Use these Reviews to find out if you need to review any of the lessons before continuing.

Performance Assessment At the end of every book, there is a special section called the Performance Assessment. This section is similar to the TABE test. It has the same number and type of questions. This assessment will give you an idea of what the real test is like.

Answer Sheet At the back of the book is a practice bubble-in answer sheet. Practice bubbling in your answers. Fill in the answer sheet carefully. For each answer, mark only one numbered space on the answer sheet. Mark the space beside the number that corresponds to the question. Mark only one answer per question. On the real TABE, if you have more than one answer per question, they will be scored as incorrect. Be sure to erase any stray marks.

Strategies and Hints Pay careful attention to the TABE Strategies and Hints throughout this book. Strategies are test-taking tips that help you do better on the test. Hints give you extra information about a skill.

Setting Goals

On the following page is a form to help you set your goals. Setting goals will help you get more from your work in this book.

Section 1. Why do you want to do well on the TABE? Take some time now to set your short-term and long-term goals on page 3.

Section 2. Making a schedule is one way to set priorities. Deadlines will help you stay focused on the steps you need to take to reach your goals.

Section 3. Your goals may change over time. This is natural. After a month, for example, check the progress you've made. Do you need to add new goals or make any changes to the ones you have? Checking your progress on a regular basis helps you reach your goals.

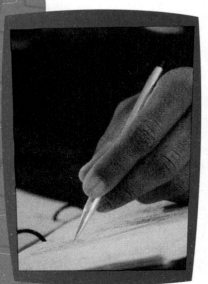

For more information on setting goals, see Steck-Vaughn's *Start Smart Goal Setting Strategies*.

1. Set Your Goals

What is your long-term goal for using this book?

_____

_____

_____

_____

Complete these areas to identify the smaller steps to take to reach your long-term goal.

Content area	What I Know	What I Want to Learn
Reading	_____	_____
Language	_____	_____
Spelling	_____	_____
Math	_____	_____
Other	_____	_____

2. Make a Schedule

Set some deadlines for yourself.

For a 20-week planning calendar, see Steck-Vaughn's *Start Smart Planner.*

Goals	Begin Date	End Date
_____	_____	_____
_____	_____	_____
_____	_____	_____
_____	_____	_____
_____	_____	_____

3. Celebrate Your Success

Note the progress you've made. If you made changes in your goals, record them here.

_____

_____

_____

_____

_____

To the Instructor

About TABE

The Tests of Adult Basic Education are designed to meet the needs of adult learners in ABE programs. Written and designed to be relevant to adult learners' lives and interests, this material focuses on the life, job, academic, and problem-solving skills that the typical adult needs.

Because of the increasing importance of thinking skills in any curriculum, *TABE Fundamentals* focuses on critical thinking throughout each TABE Objective.

The TABE identifies the following thinking processes as essential to learning and achieving goals in daily life:

- ✦ Gather Information
- ✦ Organize Information
- ✦ Analyze Information
- ✦ Generate Ideas
- ✦ Synthesize Elements
- ✦ Evaluate Outcomes

Test 1 Reading

The TABE measures an adult's ability to understand home, workplace, and academic texts. The ability to construct meaning from prose and visual information is also covered through reading and analyzing diagrams, maps, charts, forms, and consumer materials.

Test 2 Mathematics Computation

This test covers whole numbers, decimals, fractions, integers, percents, and algebraic expressions. Skills are carefully targeted to the appropriate level of difficulty.

Test 3 Applied Mathematics

This test emphasizes problem-solving and critical-thinking skills, with a focus on the life-skill applications of mathematics. Estimation and pattern-recognition skills also are important on this test.

Test 4 Language

The Language test focuses on writing and effective communication. Students examine writing samples that need revision, with complete-sentence and paragraph contexts for the various items. The test emphasizes editing, proofreading, and other key skills. The context of the questions are real-life settings appropriate to adults.

Test 5 Spelling

This test focuses on the words learners most typically misspell. In this way, the test identifies the spelling skills learners most need in order to communicate effectively. Items typically present high-frequency words in short sentences.

Uses of the TABE

There are three basic uses of the TABE:

Instructional

From an instructional point of view, the TABE allows instructors to assess students' entry levels as they begin an adult program. The TABE also allows instructors to diagnose learners' strengths and weaknesses in order to determine appropriate areas to focus instruction. Finally the TABE allows instructors and institutions to monitor learners' progress.

Administrative

The TABE allows institutions to assess classes in general and measure the effectiveness of instruction and whether learners are making progress.

Governmental

The TABE provides a means of assessing a school's or program's effectiveness.

The National Reporting System (NRS) and the TABE

Adult education and literacy programs are federally funded and thus accountable to the federal government. The National Reporting System monitors adult education. Developed with the help of adult educators, the NRS sets the reporting requirements for adult education programs around the country. The information collected by the NRS is used to assess the effectiveness of adult education programs and make necessary improvements.

A key measure defined by the NRS is educational gain, which is an assessment of the improvement in learners' reading, writing, speaking, listening, and other skills during their instruction. Programs assess educational gain at every stage of instruction.

NRS Functioning Level	Grade Level	TABE (7/8 and 9/10) scale scores
Beginning ABE Literacy	0–1.9	Reading . . . . 367 and below Total Math. . . . . 313 and below Language. . . . . . 392 and below
Beginning Basic Education	2–3.9	Reading . . . . 368–460 Total Math. . . . . 314–441 Language. 393–490
Low Intermediate Basic Education	4–5.9	Reading . . . . 461–517 Total Math. . . . . 442–505 Language. 491–523
High Intermediate Basic Education	6–8.9	Reading . . . . 518–566 Total Math. . . . . 506–565 Language. 524–559
Low Adult Secondary Education	9–10.9	Reading . . . . 567–595 Total Math. . . . . 566–594 Language. 560–585

According to the NRS guidelines, states select the method of assessment appropriate for their needs. States can assess educational gain either through standardized tests or through performance-based assessment. Among the standardized tests typically used under NRS guidelines is the TABE, which meets the NRS standards both for administrative procedures and for scoring.

The three main methods used by the NRS to collect data are the following:

1. **Direct program reporting,** from the moment of student enrollment
2. **Local follow-up surveys,** involving learners' employment or academic goals
3. **Data matching,** or sharing data among agencies serving the same clients so that outcomes unique to each program can be identified.

Two of the major goals of the NRS are academic achievement and workplace readiness. Educational gain is a means to reaching these goals. As learners progress through the adult education curriculum, the progress they make should help them either obtain or keep employment or obtain a diploma, whether at the secondary school level or higher. The TABE is flexible enough to meet both the academic and workplace goals set forth by the NRS.

Using *TABE Fundamentals*

Adult Basic Education Placement

From the outset, the TABE allows effective placement of learners. You can use the *TABE Fundamentals* series to support instruction of those skills where help is needed.

High School Equivalency

Placement often involves predicting learners' success on the GED, the high school equivalency exam. Each level of *TABE Fundamentals* covers Reading, Language, Spelling, and Applied and Computational Math to allow learners to focus their attention where it is needed.

Assessing Progress

Each TABE skill is covered in a lesson. These lessons are grouped by TABE Objective. At the end of each TABE Objective, there is a Review. Use these Reviews to find out if the learners need to review any of the skills before continuing.

At the end of the book, there is a special section called the Performance Assessment. This section is similar to the TABE test. It has the same number and type of questions. You can use the Performance Assessment as a timed pretest or posttest with your learners, or as a more general review for the actual TABE.

Steck-Vaughn's *TABE Fundamentals* Program at a Glance

The charts on the following page provide a quick overview of the elements of Steck-Vaughn's *TABE Fundamentals* series. Use this chart to match the TABE objectives with the skill areas for each level. This chart will come in handy whenever you need to find which objectives fit the specific skill areas you need to cover.

TABE OBJECTIVE	Level M		Level D		Level A
	Reading	Language and Spelling	Reading	Language and Spelling	Reading, Language, and Spelling
Reading					
Interpret Graphic Information	◆		◆		◆
Words in Context	◆		◆		◆
Recall Information	◆		◆		◆
Construct Meaning	◆		◆		◆
Evaluate/Extend Meaning	◆		◆		◆
Language					
Usage		◆		◆	◆
Sentence Formation		◆		◆	◆
Paragraph Development		◆		◆	◆
Punctuation and Capitalization		◆		◆	◆
Writing Conventions		◆		◆	◆
Spelling					
Vowels		◆		◆	◆
Consonants		◆		◆	◆
Structural Units		◆		◆	◆

TABE OBJECTIVE	Level M		Level D		Level A
	Math Computation	Applied Math	Math Computation	Applied Math	Computational and Applied Math
Mathematics Computation					
Addition of Whole Numbers	◆				
Subtraction of Whole Numbers	◆				
Multiplication of Whole Numbers	◆		◆		
Division of Whole Numbers	◆		◆		
Decimals	◆		◆		◆
Fractions	◆		◆		◆
Integers			◆		◆
Percents			◆		◆
Orders of Operation			◆		◆
Applied Mathematics					
Numbers and Number Operations		◆		◆	◆
Computation in Context		◆		◆	◆
Estimation		◆		◆	◆
Measurement		◆		◆	◆
Geometry and Spatial Sense		◆		◆	◆
Data Analysis		◆		◆	◆
Statistics and Probability		◆		◆	◆
Patterns, Functions, Algebra		◆		◆	◆
Problem Solving and Reasoning		◆		◆	◆

Lesson 1 Nominative and Relative Pronouns

Pronouns are stand-ins for nouns. You use them so that you do not have to repeat the same nouns over and over again. There are different kinds of pronouns. Pronouns can be singular or plural. They may refer to people or to things. A pronoun can be the subject of a sentence. Some pronouns link parts of sentences and show a relationship between the two parts. When you take the TABE, you will need to know how to choose pronouns correctly.

Example **Read the sentence. Which pronoun should fill in the blank: *I* or *Me*?**

Do you shop at the Grocery Barn supermarket? _____ just had a bad experience there.

I is correct. The missing word is the subject of the second sentence. Nominative pronouns serve as subjects: *I, you*, *he*, *she*, *it*, *we*, *they*. *Me* is not correct because *me* should not be used as a subject. It should be used as an object: "The clerk *gave me* the wrong change."

Example **Read the sentence. Which of the following should fill in the blank: *You and I,* or *You and me*?**

_____ have both had bad shopping experiences at the Grocery Barn.

Hint

Put the other person aside for a moment. Read the sentence aloud as if you were just talking about your experience. *I* had a bad shopping experience.

You and I is correct. When naming yourself and another person, always name yourself last. The blank in this sentence needs a subject to fill it. *You and me* is not correct because *me* should be used as an object, not a subject.

Example **A relative pronoun is another type of pronoun. Review the following examples.**

1. A **relative pronoun** can refer to a preceding noun or pronoun.

   The pronouns *who* and *whom* refer to people.

   The <u>clerk</u> to <u>whom</u> I spoke could not help me.

2. A relative pronoun can also link a phrase or clause to the rest of the sentence.

   The pronoun *that* refers to things, in this case, policies and procedures.

   Grocery Barn needs to develop new <u>policies and procedures</u> <u>that</u> are more customer-oriented.

Choose the word or phrase that best completes the sentence.

1 _____ shop for groceries every week at the same store.

    A Ourselves

    B My wife and I

    C My wife and me

    D Me and my wife

1 B The missing words are the subject of the sentence, so *My wife and I* is the correct complete subject of the sentence. Options A and C should not be used as subjects. Option D is not correct for two reasons: *Me* should not be used as a subject, and the writer should name himself last.

Practice

Read the passage. Look at the numbered, underlined portions. Choose the answer that is written correctly for the underlined portion.

(1)   <u>You and me</u> have been friends for a long time. Don't you agree that I am patient most of the time? Well, last week I ran out of patience.

(2)   Do you remember the grocery store <u>who</u> is at the corner of Oak
(3)   Street and First Avenue? And do you remember the nice man <u>that</u> used to own it? Well, I wish he were still there! The guy who owns it now has no sense of customer service.

    Right after I paid for my groceries, I discovered that my sugar
(4)   sack was leaking. You know what the new owner said? <u>Him</u> told me that I couldn't get another one because I had just paid for it and had probably ripped the hole myself!

1
  A You and I
  B Me and you
  C You and myself
  D Correct as it is

3
  A whom
  B which
  C who
  D Correct as it is

2
  F that
  G whom
  H whose
  J Correct as it is

4
  F He
  G She
  H They
  J Correct as it is

Check your answers on page 87.

You can always choose the correct pronouns once you recognize how the pronoun is used in the sentence. Some of the TABE questions will ask you to choose the correct pronouns for certain sentences.

Example   **Read this sentence. On the blank line in the sentence, write the pronoun that best completes the sentence:** *myself* **or** *me.*

I told _____ to calm down and think clearly.

Did you write *myself* on the line? The missing pronoun *myself* is singular. It matches the singular subject *I. Myself* is a **reflexive pronoun**: it reflects the action of the verb back to the subject. See the chart on page 98 of reflexive pronouns and examples of their use.

Example   **Read the sentence. Which pronoun best completes the sentence:** *that* **or** *those?*

I finally ordered _____ belt from the catalog.

Did you write *that*? *That* and other **demonstrative pronouns** point things out. *That* and *this* are used with singular nouns, so you would say "*that* belt." *These* and *those* are used with plural nouns, so you would say "*those* belts." A sense of distance can also be conveyed with demonstrative pronouns. When one or more things are nearby, use *this* and *these*. When they are far away, use *that* and *those*. Turn to page 98 for a chart of demonstrative pronouns and examples of their use.

Test Example

Read the sentence and look at the underlined portion. Choose the answer that is written correctly for the underlined portion.

1   You all are responsible for finding accommodations for
    yourselve.

   A   yourself

   B   yourselfs

   C   yourselves

   D   Correct as it is

TABE Strategy

Notice that the *f* changes to *ves* when forming the plural:
yourself ⟶ *yourselves.*

1 C The word *all* in the sentence indicates that *you* is plural, so the reflexive pronoun should also be plural. The plural form of *yourself* is *yourselves*. *Yourself* (option A) is incorrect here because it is singular. *Yourselfs* (option B) is an incorrect, misspelled form of *yourself*. *Yourselve* (option D) is also misspelled.

Practice

Read the passage. Look at the numbered, underlined portions. Choose the answer that is written correctly for the underlined portion.

(1)   People who experience food poisoning often tell theirselves that the infection is not serious. In fact, in most cases the infection goes
(2) away by themselves. However, one study showed that two of every 100 infected people die of food poisoning within a year of the
(3) infection. These fact definitely surprises most people.
(4)   You should ask yourselve's if you are at risk of getting food poisoning. Do you routinely wash fruits and vegetables in clean water before you eat them? Do you cook all meats thoroughly to kill bacteria? These kinds of food are a major source of infection.

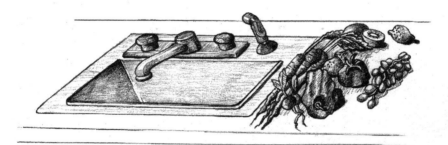

1
A themself
B himselves
C themselves
D Correct as it is

2
F itself
G itselves
H theirselves
J Correct as it is

3
A This
B Those
C Which
D Correct as it is

4
F yourself
G yourselfs
H yourselve
J Correct as it is

Check your answers on page 87.

Lesson 3 Antecedent Agreement

In all of your writing, pronouns should agree with the nouns they replace. The word a pronoun refers to is a noun, also known as an antecedent. All pronouns must agree with their antecedents in number (singular or plural). The TABE will have questions that ask you to choose sentences that use pronouns correctly.

Example **Read the sentence. What pronoun should be on the blank line?**

Jill was offered a new position after _____ job was combined with another job.

Did you write *her*? Take a look at the chart below. It shows possessive pronouns that are singular, meaning that they refer to only one person. Singular pronouns must be the same gender as the nouns they replace. The correct pronoun to replace *Jill* is *her*. Jill is one female, so the pronoun must be singular and female.

Singular Possessive Pronouns	
Male	his
Female	her, hers
Gender neutral (replaces nouns such as *house, car, book*)	its

Example **Read the sentence. What pronoun should be on the blank line?**

The company recently announced _____ decision to reorganize.

The noun *company* is gender neutral, so *its* is the correct possessive pronoun. *Its* is a pronoun that means "belonging to it." *It's* is a contraction of *it is,* which you might use in a sentence such as *It's a beautiful day!* The possessive pronoun *its* is often confused with *it's.*

Hint

Watch that apostrophe! A possessive pronoun never contains an apostrophe.

Test Example

Read the sentences. Choose the one that uses pronouns correctly.

1 A Jill felt challenged by his new position.

   B The company always announced its promotions on Fridays.

   C Karl and Jill received raises because of his new responsibilities.

   D The employees packed to prepare for his move.

1 B *Its* matches the singular noun *company*. For option A, the pronoun *his* refers to a male, so it does not match *Jill*. For option C, the pronoun *his* is singular, so it does not match the subject *Karl and Jill*. For option D, the pronoun *his* is singular, so it does not match the plural noun *employees*.

Read each group of four sentences. Choose the one that uses pronouns correctly.

1
A In today's world, many employees must face changes in her lives.

B Jill had to take a new job because of changes in her old one.

C The company was trying to keep all his employees working.

D Karl and John felt lucky that his new position was available.

2
F Jill was ready to meet with his new staff.

G Karl and John had already worked with many of her new staff.

H The company provided its employees with training.

J Karl and Jill both started his new jobs with a sense of confidence.

3
A Jill was concerned about his new health-care plan.

B Many companies are giving their employees new insurance plans.

C The plans cover employees while reducing the cost of his health care.

D Jill and Karl received a complex new insurance policy from his employer.

4
F Many people today are concerned about the cost of her health care.

G A health plan usually includes a booklet that lists their benefits.

H Fortunately, Karl's policy covers her wife and two daughters.

J Karl did not have to change his doctors.

5
A Karl tries to keep his family's medical bills down.

B His daughters do not often have to visit her pediatrician.

C Karl and his family work every day to keep its good health.

D He and his wife like to take long walks around his neighborhood.

6
F Jill exercises every day to maintain his good health.

G She carefully chooses the most healthful foods for her meals.

H Jill's parents are worried about his own health and well-being.

J Her mother and father appreciate Jill's help in her everyday lives.

Check your answers on page 87.

A verb is a word that shows action. The tense of a verb tells *when* an action takes place. The **present tense** indicates that something happens or exists now. The **future tense** refers to something that will happen in the future. On the TABE, you will be asked to choose the correct tense of different verbs.

Example **Read the sentence and write the correct verb to complete it. Should it be** *cheer* **(present tense) or** *will cheer* **(future tense)?**

I eagerly _____ for my team at the game.

Did you write *cheer*? The context of the sentence indicates that the action is happening now, so the verb should be in the present tense: *cheer*.

Note that when the subject of a sentence is a name, an object, or the pronoun *he* or *it*, an *s* is added to the end of a present tense verb. For example: *Nate cheers. The bench falls over. He picks it up. It tips over again.*

Example **Read the sentence. Notice the tense of the first verb. Should the second verb be *cheer or will cheer*? Write your answer on the blank line in the sentence.**

We have tickets for next week's game, so we _____ with all the other fans in the stands.

Did you write *will cheer*? The first verb in the sentence, *have,* is in present tense. We *have* the tickets now. However, the words *next week's game* tell you that the next action happens in the future, so the second verb should be in the future tense: *will cheer*.

Test Example

Read the sentence. Choose the verb that best completes it.

1 Joseph plans to go to the game with us, even though he also _____ to study today.

   A need

   B needs

   C needed

   D will need

TABE Strategy

When a sentence in a test item has two verbs, read it carefully to determine the correct tense of each verb.

1 **B** The verb in the first part of the sentence is in present tense. The word *also* indicates that another action will happen in the present. So the second verb should be in the present tense: he *needs* to study. The verb in option A is not in the correct form for the subject, *he*. Option C shows a past tense verb. Option D shows a future tense verb.

For numbers 1 and 2, read the paragraph and look at the numbered, underlined portions. Choose the answer that shows the correct verb tense for the underlined portion.

(1)   When Maria creates a garden, she <u>begin</u> with a plan. First she decides whether she will plant vegetables or flowers. Then she chooses
(2)   where she <u>place</u> the tall and short plants.

1 A begins
B began
C will begin
D Correct as it is

2 F places
G placed
H will place
J Correct as it is

For numbers 3 and 4, choose the sentence that uses verb tenses correctly.

3 A Her garden grow well if the weather stays warm and sunny.
B Maria will plant a vegetable garden, and her mom plant flowers.
C Her family love homemade tomato sauce, so she buys many tomato plants.
D She buys several varieties of tomatoes, and she puts each kind in a separate row.

4 F This summer James tries to outdo last year's garden successes.
G James is planning a flower garden that lined his front sidewalk.
H All winter he will study seed catalogs, so now he will be ready with his order.
J Last summer he grew lilies that everyone in the neighborhood admired.

For numbers 5 and 6, choose the verb that best completes the sentence.

5 Maria figures that she _____ money on her food bill by growing her own vegetables.
A save
B saves
C will save
D will saves

6 James does not save money on his flower garden, but he _____ it just the same.
F will enjoy
G enjoy
H enjoyed
J enjoys

Check your answers on page 87.

Perfect and Progressive Tenses

The tense of a verb tells when an action takes place. All perfect and progressive tenses require helping verbs, such as *has, have,* or *had.* A helping verb must agree with its subject in number.

Example   **Read the sentence. Then circle the correct verb to complete it.**

> Before the layoffs, Timothy _____ for the company for nearly ten years.

> works   had worked   is working   are working

Did you circle *had worked*? The words *for nearly ten years* suggest that this action took place in the past, so *had worked* is the best of the available choices. This sentence is in the perfect tense. See page 98 for a chart explaining how to form perfect tenses.

Example   **Read the sentence. Then circle the correct verb to complete it.**

> Sara _____ for the test since yesterday.

> has been studying   is studying

Did you circle *has been studying*? The progressive tense indicates that an action is ongoing. Sara is continuing to study for the test. A chart on page 98 shows how to form progressive tenses.

Test Example

Read the sentence and look at the underlined portion. Choose the answer that is written correctly for the underlined portion.

1   For decades, scientists <u>had realized</u> that loud noises can damage our hearing.

   A   has realized

   B   have realized

   C   will have realized

   D   Correct as it is

---

1   B The verb *have realized* indicates that the action began in the past, decades ago, and continues today. Option A is not correct because *scientists* is plural and *has* is singular. *Will have realized* (option C) is future perfect. *Had realized* (option D) indicates that the action is over.

For numbers 1 through 4, read the passage and look at the numbered, underlined portions. Choose the answer that is written correctly for the underlined portion.

(1)   Recent studies <u>has shown</u> that loud noises can damage the hearing of
(2)   fish. The sounds made by underwater oil exploration <u>are caused</u> this kind of
(3)   damage. One scientist said, "We <u>shouldn't a been</u> surprised about this
       finding. Loud noises hurt the hearing of mammals, so it makes sense that
       they hurt fish, too."
(4)   Oil explorers <u>will have used</u> air guns to send intense sound pulses
       through the water to the ocean floor. They analyze the returning echoes to
       learn about possible oil deposits under the ocean floor. The air guns can
       cause permanent damage to the hearing of the fish.

1
  A shown
  B were shown
  C have shown
  D Correct as it is

3
  A shouldn't been
  B should not of been
  C should not have been
  D Correct as it is

2
  F are causing
  G will be causing
  H will have caused
  J Correct as it is

4
  F had used
  G are using
  H will be using
  J Correct as it is

Check your answers on page 88.

Lesson 6   Subject and Verb Agreement

Subjects and verbs must agree, or match, in number. A singular subject requires a singular verb, while a plural subject requires a plural verb. This rule seems simple to follow, but when additional words come between the subject and verb in a sentence, some writers lose track of the subject of the sentence. This lesson will help you identify the subjects of sentences and make sure that your subjects and verbs agree.

Example   **Read the sentence. Then circle the verb that correctly completes it.**

> Thieves on the Internet _____ getting better at stealing people's identities.
>
> are   is

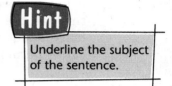

Hint

Underline the subject of the sentence.

Did you circle *are*? The subject of this sentence is *Thieves*, which is plural. The correct verb is plural: *are*. Don't be confused by the words that come between the subject and the verb. *Internet* is not the subject of the sentence.

Example   **Read the sentence. Fill in the blank with the verb that correctly completes it: *is, were, have been,* or *are*.**

> Identity theft _____ a growing problem in the United States.

The singular subject *theft* calls for the singular verb *is*. *Were, have been,* and *are* are plural.

Test Example

Read the passage and look at the numbered, underlined portion. Then choose the answer that is written correctly for the underlined portion.

(1)   If you know someone who <u>has been</u> the victim of identity theft, there are steps that person can take to stop the crime and repair his or her credit.

1   A   are

     B   were

     C   have been

     D   Correct as it is

1   D The singular subject *someone* calls for the singular verb *has been*. Options A, B, and C are plural.

Read the passage and look at the numbered, underlined portions. Choose the answer that is written correctly for the underlined portion.

(1)   How can you catch an identity thief? One of the best ways <u>is</u> to regularly check your credit record to make sure that the

(2)   information on it <u>are</u> correct.

     In addition, routinely check to determine that you are receiving all of your credit card bills. If you do not receive and review these

(3)   bills, you will not realize that someone else <u>have</u> charged purchases to your accounts.

(4)   You might be wondering how thieves <u>makes</u> charges on an account. First, they call your credit card company, pretending to

(5)   be you. Then they <u>change</u> the mailing address of your bill without

(6)   your knowledge. By the time you <u>notices</u> that you are not receiving the bill, the thieves have used your card to make some major purchases.

1
A are
B were
C have been
D Correct as it is

2
F is
G were
H have been
J Correct as it is

3
A has
B were
C have been
D Correct as it is

4
F make
G has made
H has been made
J Correct as it is

5
A changes
B is changing
C has changed
D Correct as it is

6
F notice
G has noticed
H was noticing
J Correct as it is

FIRST NATIONAL BANK

0987 6543 2109 8765

VALID THRU ▶ 12/09

KIMBERLY A SHOPPER

Check your answers on page 88.

Lesson 7 Easily Confused Verbs

Some words are easily confused, including *accept/except* and *set/sit*. Verbs that are easily confused sound alike but have different meanings. The TABE will ask you to identify the correct use of easily confused verbs.

Example   **Read the sentence. Underline the word in parentheses that correctly completes the sentence.**

I will be at work every day (except/accept) Thursday.

Did you underline *except*? *Except* means "but." Thus, "every day *except* Thursday" means "every day but Thursday." *Accept* means "to receive something willingly." For example: I gladly *accept* your gift.

Example   **Read the sentence. Underline the word in parentheses that correctly completes the sentence.**

I love to (sit/set) and watch the sun rise over the mountain peaks.

Did you underline *sit*? *Sit* means "to rest on your rear end," so it makes sense to sit and watch the sun rise. *Set* means to put something someplace. The verb *set* should always have an object, or a thing that is being put someplace. For example: I *set* the <u>box</u> on the table.

Test Example

Read the sentences. Choose the sentence that is written correctly.

1   A   The delivery person asked if I would except the package.

    B   Our company has a strict procedure on accepting packages.

    C   It seems that everyone in our office accept me knew the procedure.

    D   I excepted the package without following the procedure.

1   **B**   *Accepting* means "receiving," so option B is written correctly. Option A is not correct because *except* should be *accept*: "*if I would accept* (receive) *the package.*" Option C is incorrect because *accept* should be *except*: "*everyone except* (but) *me.*" Option D is not correct because *excepted* should be *accepted*: "*I accepted* (received) *the package.*"

Read each group of four sentences. Choose the sentence that is written correctly.

1
A Do your children take turns sitting the table at your house?

B Do they forget to sit out the salad dressing and other condiments?

C Then do they always argue over who is going to set in each chair?

D At our house, each family member sits in a certain chair.

2
F Everyone accept our toddler helps get ready for dinner.

G At the beginning of every month, everyone accepts a job.

H No one accept the parents can trade jobs with someone else.

J The children usually except their tasks cheerfully and do them well.

3
A After dinner, we sometimes set around and play games.

B On rainy days, the children love to sit up an obstacle course.

C They set large, empty boxes in a row and crawl through them.

D We do not let the children spend much time setting in front of the TV.

4
F John is the youngest person in our office accept for Cynthia.

G Still, John is ready and willing to except new responsibilities.

H Everyone except John has completed the company training program.

J Fortunately, the entire staff seems to except John as a valuable employee.

5
A John has set high standards for himself.

B He does not like to set around and take it easy.

C Some days he has a hard time setting through meetings.

D He likes to set in the back of the room so he can leave easily.

6
F Everyone except John is eligible for three weeks of vacation a year.

G John knew how much vacation he would get when he excepted the job.

H He excepted two weeks of vacation as part of working here.

J It does not bother him accept for on sunny days in spring.

Check your answers on page 88.

Lesson 8   Comparative and Superlative Adjectives

Adjectives are descriptive words. When skillfully used, adjectives can give life to your speaking and writing. They are also great for comparing things. **Comparative adjectives** are used to compare two things. **Superlative adjectives** are used to compare more than two things.

Example   **Read the sentence. Then circle the adjective that correctly completes it.**

Scientists keep trying to find the _____ dinosaur skeleton on Earth.

older   oldest   more old   most old

Did you circle *oldest*? This sentence compares more than two dinosaur skeletons, so it calls for the superlative adjective. It compares the dinosaur skeleton that scientists keep trying to find with all the other skeletons.
- Because *old* is a one-syllable adjective, you add *-est* to it to form the superlative, *oldest*.
- Adjectives with more than two syllables are made superlative by adding the word *most* before the base adjective.

See the chart on page 99 for some examples of superlative adjectives.

Example   **Read the sentence. Then circle the adjective that correctly completes the sentence.**

It is _____ to say *paleontologist* than to say "dinosaur scientist."

correcter   correctest   more correct   most correct

Did you circle *more correct*? This sentence compares two things, so it calls for a comparative adjective.
- Many comparative adjectives are formed by adding the ending *-er*.
- Adjectives with more than two syllables are made comparative by adding the word *more* before the base adjective.

See the chart on page 99 for some examples of comparative adjectives.

Test Example

Read the sentence and look at the underlined portion. Choose the answer that is written correctly for the underlined portion.

1   In 2001, an Australian named Dave Elliot found a skeleton of a sauropod, once the <u>most large</u> dinosaur on Earth.

A   larger

B   largest

C   more large

D   Correct as it is

Practice

For numbers 1 through 4, read the passage and look at the numbered, underlined portions. Choose the answer that is written correctly for the underlined portion.

> After Elliot located the dinosaur skeleton, he and his children
> (1) dug up some pieces of it. The <u>most big</u> piece was about 24 inches high and 20 inches wide. It was part of the dinosaur's right thighbone, or femur. Although the sauropod had huge legs, its
> (2) head was much <u>smallest</u> than you would expect. Nevertheless, the
> (3) average sauropod was <u>most massive</u> than five African elephants together.
>   After examining the pieces unearthed by Elliot, the scientists
> (4) dug holes to look for pieces of bone that were <u>deeper</u> in the ground.

1
A bigger
B biggest
C more big
D Correct as it is

2
F smaller
G more small
H most small
J Correct as it is

3
A massiver
B massivest
C more massive
D Correct as it is

4
F deepest
G more deep
H most deep
J Correct as it is

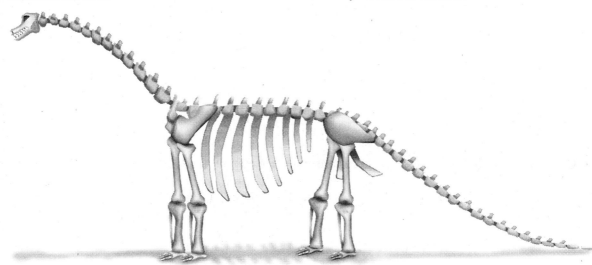

Check your answers on page 88.

Lesson 9 | Comparative Adverbs

An adverb describes a verb, adjective, or another adverb, telling how, when, where, or how much. Just as you can use adjectives to compare things, you can also use adverbs to make comparisons. Comparative adverbs are formed in much the same way that comparative adjectives are.

Example   **Read the sentence. Circle the word that correctly completes it.**

Roller-coaster rides are _____ risky than some people thought.

less   lesser   more less

Did you circle *less*? To show that one thing is "not as much" as another, you can use the adverb *less*. The missing word describes *risky*, which is an adjective. *Less risky* is correct. When making a comparison that shows a lesser degree of a quality, use *less* before the adjective or adverb.

- **Less** is an adverb that tells how little of something is done.
  I exercise less than I should.
- **Less** is also used before adverbs or adjectives to make comparisons.
  This book is less interesting than I thought it would be.

See the chart below for examples of *less* used as a comparative adverb.

Adjective or Adverb	Less as Comparative Adverb
quickly (adverb)	less quickly
contented (adjective)	less contentedly
frequently (adverb)	less frequently

Test Example

Read the sentence and look at the underlined portion. Choose the answer that is written correctly for the underlined portion.

1   Everyone agrees that riding a roller coaster is <u>more lesser</u> dangerous for people without back injuries than for people with these injuries.

   A   more less

   B   lesser

   C   less

   D   Correct as it is

1   C   The sentence is making a comparison that shows the roller coaster is not as dangerous for some people, so it requires the adverb *less*. Option A is not a comparative adverb. *Lesser* (option B) and *more lesser* (option D) are not correct comparative forms.

Read the passage and look at the numbered, underlined portions. Choose the answer that is written correctly for the underlined portion.

According to a recent study by the American Association of Neurological Surgeons, most people can ride roller coasters safely. Some people, however, ride

(1) safelier than others. The study found that injuries on these rides seem to be caused

(2) less oftener by the ride than by the riders.

The forces that people experience during

(3) the ride are lesser powerful than those required to injure a healthy person. However, these forces are still great enough

(4) to injure people who is more susceptible to

(5) injury. This will include people with neck and back injuries, pregnant women, and riders who are much shorter than the average person.

The number of injuries on all amusement

(6) park rides is lesser significant than most people think. In 2001, the rate of injury was only 2.1 for every million rides.

1
A safely
B less safely
C less safelier
D Correct as it is

2
F often
G oftener
H less often
J Correct as it is

3
A less
B more less
C more lesser
D Correct as it is

4
F were
G are
H has
J Correct as it is

5
A is including
B includes
C has included
D Correct as it is

6
F less
G more less
H most less
J Correct as it is

Check your answers on page 88.

Lesson 10 Choosing Between Adjectives and Adverbs

An adjective describes a noun or pronoun, while an adverb describes a verb, adjective, or another adverb. In this lesson, you will learn to decide whether a certain sentence requires an adjective or an adverb. You can make the correct choice by determining what the word is describing. Does it describe a noun or a pronoun—or a verb, adjective, or another adverb?

Examples **Read the sentence. Then circle the word that correctly completes it.**

Few people are _____ to receive a traffic ticket.

happy   happily

Did you circle *happy*? The word that goes in the blank describes *people*, which is a noun. This means that the missing word should be an adjective. *Happy* is an adjective; *happily* is an adverb.

Read the sentence. Then circle the correct word to complete it.

Traffic tickets must be paid _____ to avoid additional fines.

prompt   promptly

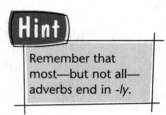

Hint

Remember that most—but not all—adverbs end in *-ly*.

Did you circle *promptly*? The word that goes in this blank describes the verb phrase *must be paid*. The missing word tells how the ticket must be paid. This means that the missing word should be an adverb. *Promptly* is an adverb, but *prompt* is an adjective.

Test Example

Read the sentence and look at the underlined portion. Choose the answer that is written correctly for the underlined portion.

1   In many communities, you can pay a traffic ticket by <u>personally</u> check, cash, or money order.

   A   personal

   B   personaller

   C   more personal

   D   Correct as it is

1   **A** The underlined word describes *check*, a noun, so the adjective *personal* is correct. Option B is not a word. Option C makes a comparison, but nothing is being compared in this sentence. *Personally* (option D) is an adverb.

For numbers 1 through 4, read the paragraphs and look at the numbered, underlined portions. Choose the answer that is written correctly for the underlined portion.

A ticket that does not involve "driving under the influence" is less
(1) <u>seriously</u> than one that does. These
(2) tickets <u>usual</u> involve speeding, lack of car insurance, or other moving
(3) violations. You can <u>quick and easily</u> send in a check or money order to pay the fines for these tickets.
A ticket for driving while intoxicated involves different rules. This violation is considered to be
(4) <u>more bad</u> than other traffic offenses.

1
A serious
B seriouser
C more serious
D Correct as it is

2
F usually
G usuallier
H more usually
J Correct as it is

3
A quick and easy
B quickly and easy
C quickly and easily
D Correct as it is

4
F worse
G badder
H more badly
J Correct as it is

For numbers 5 and 6, read the sentence and choose the words that best complete the sentence.

5 Even if you think the ticket is _____, you must pay it or go to court at the appointed date and time.
A unreasonable and unjust
B unreasonably and unjust
C unreasonably and unjustly
D unreasonable and unjustly

6 If you are _____, you can pay the fine or notify the court that you cannot appear.
F injured bad
G badly injured
H injured worse
J injured worsely

Check your answers on pages 88–89.

Lesson 11 Using Negatives

A negative is any word, including the words listed in the box below, that means "no" or "not." Good writers avoid putting two negatives in the same sentence. If you use negatives sparingly, your writing will be easier to understand. The box below includes many common negative words.

Negatives	
no	neither
not	nothing
none	nobody
never	hardly
nowhere	scarcely
no one	barely

Example **Read the sentence. Then circle the words that best complete it.**

My brother _____ to charities.

doesn't never give anything

does not ever give anything

does not ever give nothing

Hint

Watch for contractions with *not* in them, such as *couldn't* or *shouldn't*.

Did you circle *does not ever give anything*? This is the only choice with only one negative in it. *Doesn't* and *never* are both negatives, and so are *not* and *nothing*.

Test Example

Read the sentences and look at the underlined portion. Choose the answer that is written correctly for the underlined portion.

1 Do you wonder where the money goes when people give to charities? In some cases, <u>not none</u> of it goes where it is supposed to go.

    A none

    B scarcely none

    C not nothing

    D Correct as it is

1 **A** This option has only one negative. Option B has two negatives, *scarcely* and *none*. Option C has two negatives, *not* and *nothing*. Option D has two negatives, *not* and *none*.

Read the passage and look at the numbered, underlined portions. Choose the answer that is written correctly for the underlined portion.

Here are some ways to figure out which charities are legitimate and worthy of your help.

(1) • Ask the person at the door or on the phone for identification. A professional fund-raiser <u>will not hardly refuse</u> to give you this information.

(2) • Ask how the money will be used. A legitimate organization <u>won't be surprised</u> at this request.

(3) • Do not give money for a pledge you <u>don't never remember</u> making.

(4) • <u>Do not scarcely be fooled</u> by names. Some phony groups use names that are very similar to names of respected national charities.

(5) • Remember that if you get a gift for your donation, it <u>isn't in no way free.</u> Part of your donation will be used to pay for that "gift."

(6) • <u>Do not never let yourself be pressured</u> into making a decision. If you have to decide right then, say "no."

1
A will hardly refuse
B won't hardly refuse
C will not never refuse
D Correct as it is

2
F won't never be surprised
G will not never be surprised
H will hardly not be surprised
J Correct as it is

3
A do not remember
B cannot barely remember
C can't hardly at all remember
D Correct as it is

4
F Do not never be fooled
G Don't be fooled none
H Don't be fooled
J Correct as it is

5
A isn't in any way free
B is not free neither
C isn't never free
D Correct as it is

6
F Don't let no one pressure you
G Don't be pressured by no one
H Never be pressured
J Correct as it is

Check your answers on page 89.

For numbers 1 through 8, read the passage and look at the numbered, underlined portions. Choose the answer that is written correctly for the underlined portion.

Making the Most of a Job Interview

(1)   Many jobs <u>is</u> filled by having applicants complete a job interview. The

(2)   interview is <u>usual</u> handled by someone in the company's human resources

department or by the person who will supervise the new employee.

(3)   During the interview you want to give a good first impression of <u>yourselve</u>

(4)   and get more information about the job and the company. <u>Do not never</u> sit

down before you are asked to do so. Try not to show signs of nervousness,

(5)   such as fidgeting or tensing up. <u>These</u> kinds of behavior will make you look

(6)   bad. After the interview <u>will had started</u>, you will probably feel more

comfortable.

After the interview, be sure to send a thank-you letter. In the letter, re-

(7)   state your interest in the position. Be sure to thank the person <u>that</u>

(8)   interviewed you for his or her time. Impressive candidates <u>mails</u> their thank-

you letters within a day after the interview.

1 **A** are	**5** **A** This
B was	**B** That
C has been	**C** Which
D Correct as it is	**D** Correct as it is
2 **F** usually	**6** **F** has started
G usualler	**G** had started
H more usual	**H** was started
J Correct as it is	**J** Correct as it is
3 **A** yourselves	**7** **A** what
B yourself	**B** which
C ourself	**C** who
D Correct as it is	**D** Correct as it is
4 **F** Don't never	**8** **F** will mail
G Do not ever	**G** mail
H Don't under no conditions	**H** mailed
J Correct as it is	**J** Correct as it is

For numbers 9 through 12, choose the sentence that is written correctly.

9
  A The interviewer will ask many questions, and you will answer each one.

  B Your body language had showed your level of comfort during the interview.

  C Interviews will get easier after you had more experience with them.

  D The interviewer will starts with easy questions so you feel more comfortable.

10
  F You can ask questions about almost anything accept the job salary.

  G As you sit, lean forward slightly to show interest in the interview.

  H Sit your handbag or briefcase on the floor beside your chair.

  J At the end, you might be asked to except the job.

11
  A Henry and David have updated his resumes.

  B Most job applicants should bring resumes to her interviews.

  C The interviewer and other people may want copies for his files.

  D A company may conduct many interviews for just one of its positions.

12
  F I have been preparing for my interview all day.

  G You has been helping me prepare for my interview.

  H You have been help all day.

  J They has been making me very nervous.

For numbers 13 through 16, read the sentence and choose the word or phrase that best completes the sentence.

13 In some cases, your qualifications are _____ important than your attitude.

  A less

  B more less

  C most less

  D very

14 The interviewer to _____ you should speak is in a meeting right now.

  F who

  G what

  H whom

  J which

15 _____ could help each other practice interviewing.

  A I and you

  B You and I

  C Me and you

  D You and me

16 If you prepare yourself, you can do well on even the _____ interview.

  F difficulter

  G difficultest

  H most difficult

  J more difficult

Check your answers on page 89.

Lesson 12 Sentence Recognition

Good writers use complete sentences. Sometimes writers forget to include all of the necessary parts of speech or punctuation. Sometimes a group of words is missing a subject or a verb. Sometimes sentences are joined without the correct punctuation. A chart on page 99 outlines rules for recognizing complete sentences, run-on sentences, and sentence fragments.

Example **Read the group of words. Then circle the term that describes it.**

> Many people could cut their transportation costs they could walk more and drive less.

> complete sentence   fragment   run-on

Did you circle *run-on*? This is two sentences run together as one. The first sentence ends after *costs*, where there should be a period. The second sentence should begin with the word *They*.

Test Example

Read the sentence and look at the underlined portion. Choose the answer that is written correctly for the underlined portion.

1   Be sure to change your car's oil and air filters at the recommended <u>times doing</u> it yourself can cut costs.

  A   times, doing

  B   times doing,

  C   times. Doing

  D   Correct as it is

Hint

As you read a sentence, circle all the subjects and underline all the verbs. If there are two or more subject-verb pairs marked, it could be a run-on sentence.

1   **C**   This run-on needs to be divided into two sentences. A comma (option A) does not divide the run-on into two sentences. The comma in option B does not divide the run-on into two sentences and is not positioned correctly between the two sentences. As it is (option D), this group of words is a run-on.

For numbers 1 through 4, choose the sentence that is written correctly and shows the correct capitalization and punctuation.

1

A One way to cut costs is to take better care of your car a well-maintained automobile is safer and less expensive to drive.

B You can cut your transportation costs in a number of ways.

C The instructions in your car owner's manual.

D Operating more efficiently for more miles.

2

F Auto repair classes in your community.

G Much of the expense of maintaining an automobile.

H Doing your own maintenance can reduce costs significantly.

J Form car pools find neighbors who work in the same part of town.

3

A Unnecessary repair bills in the future.

B Find gas stations with self-service pumps.

C The cost of insurance, taxes, and maintenance.

D Keep your car clean protect it against salt damage and rust.

4

F Oil and water levels in the engine.

G Good driving habits, such as slowing down gradually.

H Locate gas stations that sell good-quality gas at low prices.

J Get gas when you pass by one of these stations don't make a special trip.

For numbers 5 and 6, read the paragraph below and look at the numbered, underlined portions. Choose the answer that is written correctly for each underlined portion.

(5)   You might carry just liability coverage on an older <u>automobile for</u> this car, collision and comprehensive coverage might not

(6)   make sense. After an accident it might not <u>pay to</u> have an older car repaired.

5

A automobile for,

B automobile, for

C automobile. For

D Correct as it is

6

F pay; to

G pay, to

H pay. To

J Correct as it is

Check your answers on page 90.

Lesson 13 | Adding Modifiers to Combine Sentences

Modifiers are descriptive words. Too many short sentences make writing choppy and hard to read. You can combine some short sentences by taking a few modifiers from one sentence and adding them to another one. They turn simple sentences into more specific ones.

Example **Read these sentences. Write a sentence that combines the information**

from both sentences. _____

Sentence 1 An accident made the traffic even worse.
Sentence 2 The accident was at Elm and First Streets.

You probably wrote something like this: "An accident at Elm and First Streets made the traffic even worse." The phrase _at Elm and First Streets_ in the second sentence tells where the accident was. By adding it to the first sentence, you create a single, strong sentence.

Example **Read these sentences. Write a sentence that combines the information**

from both sentences. _____

Sentence 1 I remembered the license plate number and was able
to report it to the police.
Sentence 2 I clearly remembered the license plate number.

You probably wrote something like this: "I clearly remembered the license plate number and was able to report it to the police." These sentences are best combined by moving the adverb _clearly_ from the second sentence into the first sentence.

Test Example

Read the underlined sentences. Choose the sentence that best combines the sentences.

1   July was a hot month.
It was windy in July.
It was humid in July.

   A   July was a hot, humid, windy, weather month.

   B   July was a hot, windy, and humid month.

   C   July was a hot month, and it was windy and humid.

   D   July was a hot month, with windy, humid weather.

TABE Strategy

Read each answer choice and check whether it has the same meaning as the original sentences.

1   **B**   This sentence includes the adjectives _windy_ and _humid_ from the second and third sentences to create one strong, single sentence. Options A and D use the word _weather,_ which is not in any of the original sentences. Option C uses extra unnecessary words.

Read the underlined sentences. Choose the sentence that best combines the sentences.

1 We drove through the traffic to her office.

The traffic was heavy.

A We drove through the heavy traffic to her office.

B Heavy, we drove through the traffic to her office.

C The traffic was heavy when we drove through it to her office.

D We drove through the traffic to her office, but the traffic was heavy.

2 Pollution can make it hard to breathe.

The pollution comes from cars, trucks, and buses.

F Pollution can make it hard to breathe from cars, trucks, and buses.

G Pollution from cars, trucks, and buses can make it hard to breathe.

H Pollution can make it hard for cars, trucks, and buses to breathe.

J Cars, trucks, and buses can make it hard to breathe.

3 Because of poor air quality, city officials announced a smog alert.

This happened on television.

A Because of poor air quality, city officials announced a smog alert, and this was on television.

B Because of poor air quality, city officials announced a smog alert on television.

C Because of poor air quality on television, city officials announced a smog alert.

D Because of poor air quality, city officials announced on television smog alert.

4 My sister has an asthma condition that is made worse by air pollution.

Her condition is serious.

F My sister has a serious asthma condition that is made worse by air pollution.

G My sister has an asthma condition that is made worse by serious air pollution.

H My sister has an asthma condition that is made seriously worse by air pollution.

J My sister has an asthma condition that is made worse by air pollution, and it is serious.

5 Outside my office window, I could see particles of soot in the air.

The particles were tiny.

The particles were also dark.

A Outside my office window, I could see tiny particles of soot in the dark air.

B Outside my office window, I could see tiny, dark particles of soot in the air.

C Outside my office window, I could see particles of soot in the tiny, dark air.

D Outside my office window, I could see particles of soot in the air that were tiny and dark.

Check your answers on page 90.

Too many short sentences make writing choppy and hard to read. The TABE asks you to combine pairs of short, related sentences. If the verbs of both sentences are very similar, you can combine the subjects with the word *and* and state the verb only once. This is called compounding. Compounding sentences makes your writing more interesting and less repetitive.

Example **Read these two sentences. The verbs are the same, so you can combine the sentences by joining the subjects and stating the verb just once. Write your new sentence.** _____

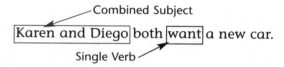

Subjects
Karen wants a new car. Diego wants a new car, too.
Verbs

You probably wrote something like this: "Karen and Diego both want a new car." Karen and Diego are combined with *and* to form a combined subject. The verb in both sentences is *want*, so the verb is stated just once. Look at the combined sentence below. It shows the compound subject and single verb.

Combined Subject
Karen and Diego both want a new car.
Single Verb

Test Example

Read the underlined sentences. Choose the sentence that best combines those sentences into one.

1   Carlos is always looking for low-cost activities to do with his children.

Julia also looks for low-cost activities to do with her children.

A   Carlos and Julia, they like to do low-cost activities with their children.

B   Carlos looks and Julia also looks for low-cost activities to do with their children.

C   Carlos and Julia are always looking for low-cost activities to do with their children.

D   Carlos is always looking for low-cost activities to do with his children, and Julia looks for low-cost activities to do with her children, too.

1   C This sentence combines the two subjects, *Carlos* and *Julia,* and states the verb once. Option A states the subjects and then adds the pronoun *they,* which should take the place of a subject. Option B repeats the verb *looks* and sounds awkward. Option D unnecessarily repeats many words.

Read the underlined sentences. Choose the sentence that best combines those sentences into one.

1 Zoos often cost less on certain days.

Children's museums also cost less on certain days.

A Zoos and children's museums often cost less on certain days.

B Zoos and children's museums, they often cost less on certain days.

C Zoos often cost less and children's museums also cost less on certain days.

D Zoos often cost less on certain days, and children's museums also cost less on certain days, too.

2 The Hunt Library offers free concerts and story times for children.

The North Library also offers free concerts and story times for children.

F Two libraries offer free concerts and story times for children.

G The Hunt and North Libraries offer free concerts and story times for children.

H The Hunt Library offers free concerts, and the North Library offers free story times for children.

J The Hunt Library offers free concerts and story times for children, and the North Library offers free concerts and story times for children, too.

3 Many parents take their children to the park.

Many grandparents also take their grandchildren to the park.

A Many parents take their children to the park, and many grandparents do, too.

B Many parents and grandparents take their children or grandchildren to the park.

C Many parents and grandparents take their children to the park.

D Many parents take their children to the park, and many grandparents take their grandchildren to the park, too.

4 The Community Center is offering swimming lessons this summer.

A local swimming club is also offering swimming lessons this summer.

F The Community Center and a local swimming club are offering swimming lessons this summer.

G The Community Center and a local swimming club, they are offering swimming lessons this summer.

H The Community Center is offering swimming lessons this summer, and so is a local swimming club.

J The Community Center is offering swimming lessons this summer, and a local swimming club is offering swimming lessons this summer, too.

5 Julia takes her children to swimming lessons at the Community Center.

Carlos takes his children to swimming lessons at the Community Center.

A Julia and Carlos both take their children to swimming lessons at the Community Center.

B Julia takes and Carlos takes their children to swimming lessons at the Community Center.

C Julia takes her children to swimming lessons, and Carlos takes his children to the Community Center.

D Julia takes her children to swimming lessons at the Community Center, and Carlos takes his children to swimming lessons at the Community Center.

Check your answers on page 90.

There are many ways to combine short, choppy sentences. This lesson will help you learn two more sentence combination methods that you can use in the TABE and in your everyday writing.

Example **Read these two sentences. Combine them with one of these words:** *and,* *or, so,* **or** *but.* _____

_____

Sentence 1 Benji's class is from 7:00 to 9:00 p.m. two nights a week.

Sentence 2 He has found a job during the day at a restaurant.

You probably wrote something like this: "Benji's class is from 7:00 to 9:00 p.m. two nights a week, so he has found a job during the day at a restaurant." You have created a stronger sentence by joining the two shorter sentences with the word *so.*

Test Example

Read the underlined sentences. Choose the sentence that best combines those sentences into one.

1 Renee plans to go to school during the day.

She hopes to earn a two-year degree.

A Renee plans to go to school during the day or earn a two-year degree.

B Renee plans to go to school and earn a two-year degree.

C Renee, who hopes to earn a two-year degree, plans to go to school during the day.

D Renee plans to go to school during the day, so she hopes to earn a two-year degree.

> **TABE Strategy**
>
> Read all the answer choices before selecting the best one.

> **1 C** This option combines the two sentences without changing the meaning. Option A makes going to school and earning a degree seem like two different tasks. Option B leaves out *during the day.* In option D the word *so* combines the sentences in a confusing way.

Read the underlined sentences. Choose the sentence that best combines those sentences into one.

1 Christopher completed a two-year program at a trade school.

He is now an electrician.

A Christopher completed a two-year program at a trade school as an electrician.

B Christopher, who is now an electrician, completed a two-year program at a trade school.

C Christopher completed a two-year program at a trade school, but he is now an electrician.

D Christopher is the one who completed a two-year program at a trade school, and he is now an electrician.

2 Many young people want to get into the workforce as quickly as possible.

That's why they go to trade schools.

F Many young people want to get into the workforce as quickly as possible, but they go to trade schools.

G Many young people want to get into the workforce as quickly as possible, so they go to trade schools.

H Many young people want to get into the workforce as quickly as possible, or they go to trade schools.

J Getting into the workforce as quickly as possible, many young people want to go to trade schools.

3 Some students at trade schools learn a new trade.

Other students learn how to use the latest technology in their own trade.

A Some students at trade schools learn a new trade, and others learn how to use the latest technology in their own trade.

B Since students at trade schools learn a new trade, others learn how to use the latest technology in their own trade.

C Students, who are at trade schools, learn how to use the latest technology in their own trade.

D Learning a new trade, students learn how to use the latest technology in their own trade.

4 Kevin wants to go to trade school and become an automotive technician.

He just graduated from high school.

F Kevin wants to go to trade school, become an automotive technician, and graduate from high school.

G Kevin, who wants to go to trade school, will become an automotive technician and graduate from high school.

H Kevin, who just graduated from high school, wants to go to trade school and become an automotive technician.

J Kevin, graduating from high school, is the one who wants to go to trade school and become an automotive technician.

Check your answers on page 90.

Lesson 16 Misplaced Modifiers

When you read a sentence and can't tell what word describes what, the problem is usually a misplaced modifier. A **modifier** is a word or phrase that alters the meaning of another word or phrase. Where you place a modifier makes a big difference in the meaning of a sentence. A misplaced modifier can completely change the meaning of a sentence. As a rule, you should always put modifiers next to the words they describe.

Example   Read the sentence and notice the underlined words. Do the underlined words modify *poodle* or *woman*? _____

I saw a woman walking a poodle <u>wearing a baseball cap</u>.

The underlined words incorrectly modify *poodle*, making it sound as if the poodle was wearing the baseball cap. Surely the writer intended to say that the woman was wearing the baseball cap: *I saw a woman wearing a baseball cap walking a poodle.*

Example   Read the sentence and notice the underlined word. What does the underlined word modify?

Terri <u>almost</u> spent a thousand dollars on car repairs.

The word *almost* modifies *spent*. As written, this means that Terri nearly spent the money, but for some reason didn't. In fact, what the writer means to say was that the amount Terri spent on repairing her car was close to a thousand dollars. Misplaced modifiers can be corrected by changing the word order. The sentence should read:

Terri spent <u>almost</u> a thousand dollars on car repairs.

When *almost* is closer to *a thousand dollars,* the meaning is clear: Terri's car repair bill was close to a thousand dollars.

Test Example

Read the sentence and look at the underlined portion. Choose the answer that is written correctly for the underlined portion.

1   We put the salad <u>in the refrigerator, and we planned to eat it later.</u>

A   in the refrigerator, which we planned to eat later.

B   , which we planned to eat later, in the refrigerator.

C   that we planned to eat later, we put the salad in the refrigerator.

D   Correct as it is

1   **B**   *In option A, the meaning is that they are planning to eat the refrigerator. Option C is unnecessarily wordy and is, therefore, unclear. Option D, like option A, indicates that they are planning to eat the refrigerator.*

For numbers 1 to 6, read the passage and look at the numbered, underlined portions. Circle the letter of the sentence that is written correctly for each underlined portion.

(1)   At the age of 12, Jenny's dad remarried. My wife and I were invited to the wedding. It was
(2) held on a cold day in November. Falling gently outside the window, we could see the first snowflakes of the year. The church was lit entirely with candles. Guests from all around
(3) the state attended the wedding. A soloist with a beautiful voice sang a few songs.
       After the wedding, the reception was held at a
(4) local restaurant. Walking past the food table, the wedding cake looked delicious! I had three pieces
(5) and could have eaten more. A band provided music for dancing with a great saxophone player. Some kids were teaching us older people some new dances. They were wild, but fun! My wife
(6) and I almost stayed at the reception until midnight. We didn't get home until quarter of one. As you can guess, we had a terrific time!

1
A Jenny was 12, her dad remarried.
B When Jenny was 12, her dad remarried.
C When he was 12, Jenny's dad remarried.
D Correct as it is

2
F We could see the first snowflakes of the year falling gently outside the window.
G We, falling gently outside the window, could see the first snowflakes of the year.
H We could see the first snowflakes, falling gently outside the window, of the year.
J Correct as it is

3
A sang with a beautiful voice. A few songs.
B sang a few songs with a beautiful voice.
C with a beautiful voice. Sang a few songs.
D Correct as it is

4
F The wedding cake looked delicious walking past the food table!
G We saw the wedding cake walking past the food table, and it looked delicious!
H We saw the wedding cake as we were walking past the food table, and it looked delicious!
J Correct as it is

5
A with a great saxophone player provided music for dancing.
B provided music with a great saxophone player for dancing.
C provided music for dancing. With a great saxophone player.
D Correct as it is

6
F stayed almost at the reception until midnight.
G stayed at the reception until almost midnight.
H stayed at the reception almost until midnight.
J Correct as it is

Check your answers on pages 90–91.

Lesson 17 Nonparallel Structure

Have you noticed that some sentences seem awkward, while others read smoothly? One reason for this awkwardness is a lack of parallel structure. That is, the ideas in the sentences are not explained using the same (parallel) grammatical structure. Good writers use parallel structure to make their sentences easier to read and understand.

Example Read the sentence aloud. Notice the underlined groups of words and think about how they sound. Do the two groups of words sound as though they are parallel in structure? _____

Chain letters often ask you to <u>send someone money</u> or to <u>make a phone call</u>.

The answer is yes. They do sound alike. That is because the two phrases have the same word pattern. The verbs *send* and *make* are in the same tense, and the complete phrases are in the same form. The two phrases have parallel structure.

Example Read the sentence. Then circle the group of words that best completes it.

Chain-letter requests include sending someone money or _____.

making a phone call   to make a phone call

Did you circle *making a phone call*? *Sending someone money* and *making a phone call* have parallel structure. They both begin with a verb ending in *-ing*.

Test Example

Read the sentence and look at the underlined portion. Choose the answer that is written correctly for the underlined portion.

1 Chain letters might promise that you will have good luck or <u>to get thousands of recipes.</u>

    A will get thousands of recipes

    B getting thousands of recipes

    C when you get thousands of recipes

    D Correct as it is

1 **A** *Will get thousands of recipes* has the same structure as *will have good luck*. Option B starts with a verb ending in *-ing*. Option C begins with *when*. For option D, *to get* is not the same structure as *will have*.

Read the passage and look at the numbered, underlined portions. Choose the answer that is written correctly for each underlined portion.

(1)   Nearly everyone has received or <u>to hear</u> about chain letters. The simplest chain letters contain a list and tell you to send something to the person at the top of the list, to remove that
(2)   name, and <u>adding</u> your own name to the bottom of the list. Then the letter instructs you to "continue the chain" by mailing
(3)   the letter to other people or <u>to phone</u> them.
         However, the Federal Trade Commission warns that chain
(4)   letters involving money are illegal and <u>breaking</u> the law. People who still decide to "continue the chain" usually
(5)   receive little or nothing in return, and <u>not getting rich</u>. For more information about chain letters, call the U.S. Postal
(6)   Inspection Service at 1-888-877-7644 or <u>to contact them</u> at *www.framed.usps.com / postalinspectors / chainlet.htm.*

1
A has heard
B hearing
C is hearing
D Correct as it is

2
F add
G added
H to add
J Correct as it is

3
A phone
B has phoned
C by phoning
D Correct as it is

4
F break
G broke
H to break
J Correct as it is

5
A if they do not get rich
B they do not get rich
C to not get rich
D Correct as it is

6
F when you contact them
G if you contact them
H contact them
J Correct as it is

Check your answers on page 91.

Here are some tips for successfully removing a tick. For numbers 1 through 3, read the passage and look at the numbered, underlined portions. Choose the answer that is written correctly for each underlined portion.

(1)   If you find a tick on your skin. Don't panic. It's relatively
(2)   easy to remove the tick, dispose of it, and killing any germs.
(3)   Grasping with a tissue or tweezers, the tick will come off easily.
      Then dispose of the tick by wrapping it tightly and placing it in a
      garbage can.

1   **A** skin don't

   B skin don't,

   C skin, don't

   D Correct as it is

2   **F** and kill any germs

   G and you kill any germs

   H and any germs can be killed

   J Correct as it is

3   **A** The tick will come off easily, grasping with a tissue or tweezers.

   B The tick, grasping with a tissue or tweezers, will come off easily.

   C Grasp the tick with a tissue or tweezers, and it will come off easily.

   D Correct as it is

For numbers 4 and 5, read the underlined sentences. Then choose the sentence that best combines those sentences into one.

4   Pull on the tick until it lets go.
   Pull slowly.

   F Pull on the tick until it lets go slowly.

   G Pull on the tick slowly until it lets go.

   H Pull on the tick, and it will slowly let go.

   J Pull on the tick until it lets go, and pull slowly.

5   A lighted match is not recommended for removing a tick.
   Petroleum jelly is also not recommended.

   A Neither a lighted match nor petroleum jelly is recommended for removing a tick.

   B A lighted match and petroleum jelly, they are not recommended for removing a tick.

   C A lighted match is not and petroleum jelly is not recommended for removing a tick.

   D A lighted match is not recommended for removing a tick, and petroleum jelly is also not recommended.

Check your answers on page 91.

Lesson 18 Topic Sentence

A strong paragraph begins with a topic sentence that introduces the paragraph and explains its main idea. A paragraph without a good topic sentence begins in the middle of a thought. Readers have to struggle to understand what the writer is trying to say.

Example **Read the paragraph. Then write a topic sentence on the blank line at the beginning of the paragraph.**

_____. Begin by getting referrals from your family, friends, and other doctors. Ask for names of doctors they recommend—and doctors they would avoid. A local hospital might have a list of doctors in your area. The local medical society might also offer some guidance.

One possible topic sentence is: *Here are some tips for finding a new doctor.* The paragraph lists ways to start looking for a new doctor. However, without a topic sentence, readers must finish the paragraph before they are sure of its topic.

Test Example

Read the paragraph. Then choose the sentence that best fills the blank in the paragraph.

1 _____. You might go to the library and look him or her up in the American Medical Directory, the Directory of American Specialists, or other directories. If you need help with a certain medical problem, find out how much experience and training the doctor has in that field.

    A Check on the doctor's background.

    B Go to the library if you need more information.

    C Some regions have many doctors available, while others have few.

    D Primary care physicians include family practitioners and pediatricians.

Hint

Read the paragraph and think about the main idea. Which option most closely states that idea?

1 A This is the best topic sentence because the paragraph describes ways to check a doctor's qualifications. It mentions the library (option B) only in passing. It does not discuss the number of doctors available (option C). It also does not discuss primary care physicians (option D).

Read each paragraph. Then choose the sentence that best fills the blank in the paragraph.

1 _____. Some plans have lists of doctors who are authorized to work for the plan. If you go to a doctor who is not on the list, you might have to pay most or all of the bill. If you are unsure about your coverage, call your health plan directly. If you have no health insurance, talk to the doctor's staff about payment options.

A Medical bills have skyrocketed in recent years.

B Health insurance has become increasingly complicated.

C Make sure your insurance plan covers the doctor you have chosen.

D You may have to fill out insurance forms at your first appointment.

2 _____. Schedule an interview to meet the doctor and find out whether you feel comfortable talking with this person. Is he or she a good listener and concerned about your health, or is this doctor more at ease talking about tests and medications? Does he or she look you in the eye and give you time to gather your thoughts?

F Make sure the office is clean and comfortable.

G Find out if the doctor is available in an emergency.

H If the doctor's age is important to you, find out what it is.

J The doctor's personality will directly affect your relationship.

3 _____. You might choose a pediatrician or a family physician. Pediatricians treat patients from birth through adolescence. Family physicians treat patients of all ages. It is helpful to take your child to a doctor who specializes in children. Still, there are advantages to having the same doctor treat all family members.

A There are many kinds of doctors.

B Selecting a doctor for your child can be challenging.

C Family physicians must complete three years of residency.

D Some pediatricians specialize in emergency medicine or other areas.

4 _____. When is the office open? Are there any evening or weekend hours? Whom can you contact when the office is closed? Can you communicate with your doctor through e-mail? Does a partner take over in the doctor's absence?

F How often does the doctor refer patients to specialists?

G Learn as much as you can about the doctor's practice.

H Doctors' offices can be busy places.

J What are the payment policies?

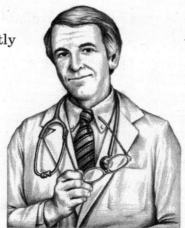

Check your answers on page 91.

Lesson 19 | Supporting Sentences

A strong paragraph begins with a topic sentence, but it also needs supporting sentences that develop or provide details about the topic. The TABE asks you to identify appropriate supporting sentences for a topic sentence. This lesson will help you strengthen that skill.

Example Read the topic sentence. Then read options A and B. Do the sentences in option A or B support the topic sentence? _____

> **Topic Sentence** Orienteering is a cross-country race in which the players use maps and compasses to find a certain spot first.
>
> **Option A** This kind of competition began in the forests of Norway in 1897. Now the International Orienteering Federation has 60 member nations.
>
> **Option B** The Chinese invented compasses long ago. By the eleventh century, Chinese ships were using compasses to navigate the seas.

The sentences in option A support the topic sentence by providing more details about orienteering. Combining this topic sentence with the supporting sentences in option A creates a stronger paragraph. The sentences in option B discuss compasses, which are just a detail in the topic sentence.

Test Example

Choose the answer that best develops the topic sentence.

1 The Orienteering Federation sponsors a competition called Park World Tour.

    A This sport allows spectators to watch up close. The race lasts about 90 minutes.

    B Orienteering can be practiced anywhere in the world. People of all ages can try it in a local park, for example.

    C Youngsters especially like this sport. The races provide lots of speed, excitement, and action.

    D Players navigate through the parks and cities of the world. Past tours have taken place in China, Japan, Norway, Finland, Italy, and many other nations.

> **1 D** The sentences in option D support the topic sentence by providing details about the Park World Tour. Options A, B, and C provide details about orienteering in general.

Choose the answer that best develops the topic sentence.

1 One important race on the 2002 Park World Tour took place in the ancient city of Matera, Italy.

A The narrow stone streets of Matera provided quite a challenge for orienteering. Some of the racers lost valuable time because of the twisting city streets.

B The world's top 25 male and female orienteers race in every Park World Tour. The organizers hope that orienteering will be an Olympic sport by 2012.

C The races take place all over the world. The idea is to increase interest in and knowledge about this sport, and to introduce it in more countries.

D The racers have maps, but they choose their own routes. Sometimes they later wish that they had selected a different route.

2 The racers must get their control cards punched at about 15 locations during the race.

F Racers start one minute apart. Each start and finish time is carefully recorded.

G The women and men compete in separate races on the same course. The fastest racers from the previous race start last.

H Spectators must remain in a certain area. They are not permitted to help the racers or give them information about the route.

J These controls ensure that racers do not take unfair shortcuts. Their cards are checked after the race to make sure that they stopped at all the control sites.

3 The Park World Tour racers compete on a course that includes both city streets and parks.

A The women complete the race in about 15 minutes. The men take about 12 minutes. Because the racers start about one minute apart, the whole event takes about 90 minutes.

B Local volunteers can join the race if some of the scheduled competitors withdraw at the last minute. These volunteers must be very good at orienteering, however.

C The course is mapped out by the host city months ahead of time. The Park World Tour organizers must approve the course before it becomes official.

D Spectators cheer wildly as the racers reach the finish line. The cheers are in many languages, as many nations send racers.

4 To learn more about the Park World Tour, watch for the races on television.

F The first Park World Tour took place in 1996. A year later, the races were attracting 5,000 spectators.

G Televised sports can be exciting. They give viewers a close-up look at the race and the racers.

H You can also check out the Park World Tour Web site. It's www.pwt.org.

J Each course covers 3 km. That's 1.86 miles, with many twists and turns.

Check your answers on page 91.

Lesson 20 Sequence

Good writers present ideas in a logical sequence. If the ideas in a paragraph are out of sequence, they are difficult to understand. The TABE asks you to choose a sentence that fits into a certain place in a paragraph. If you think about the sequence of ideas in the paragraph, you will be able to choose the correct sentence. This lesson provides practice in that skill.

Example **Read the paragraph. Should Sentence A or B fill the blank line in the paragraph?** _____

> You should check the pressure on your car tires at least once a month. _____ Use the gauge to check the tires when they are cold, that is, after the car has not been driven for at least three hours. Driving makes the air inside tires warmer, increasing the air pressure.

Sentence A You will get an accurate reading only when the tires are cold.

Sentence B First buy a tire pressure gauge and keep it in your vehicle.

Sentence B is the best choice to fill in the blank because you must buy a tire gauge before you can use it. This sentence includes the word *first*, which is a clue that it comes early in the paragraph. Sentence A does not fit in this blank because it mentions "cold" tires before the writer explains what that means. Sentence A fits at the end of the paragraph.

Test Example

Read the paragraph. Then choose the sentence that best fills the blank in the paragraph.

1　To check your tire pressure, you must first determine the recommended tire pressure for your vehicle. _____ Then record the current pressure of all the tires. If the pressure on any of them is too high, slowly press on the tire valve stem to release air.

   A   It might be a good idea to keep a permanent record of the tire pressure.

   B   You can probably find the correct tire pressure in the owner's manual.

   C   Keep pressing until the pressure returns to the recommended level.

   D   Consider checking the pressure on the same day every month.

> **TABE Strategy**
>
> Words such as *first, second, next,* and *then* can help you determine the correct sequence.

1　B This sentence explains how to find the recommended tire pressure, so it logically follows the first sentence. Options A and D are general tips unrelated to determining the recommended tire pressure. Option C should go at the end of the paragraph.

Level D

Lesson 20 • **49**

Read each paragraph. Then circle the letter of the sentence that best fills the blank in each paragraph.

1 You might find that the tire pressure is too low. If so, note the difference between the tire pressure and the recommended level. _____ You can do this at a service station.

A On some vehicles, the front and rear tires should have different amounts of pressure.

B You will need to increase the air pressure in any underinflated tires.

C You have probably noticed air pumps at service stations.

D For most cars, all tires should have the same pressure.

2 During a trip, you might notice that a tire seems to be underinflated. For example, as you stop for gas, you might notice that one tire is flatter on the bottom than the others. Most tires do lose air slowly over time. _____

F Make sure to check the air pressure before you begin a long trip.

G They can also lose air suddenly if you hit a pothole, curb, or other object.

H You can use the gauge to check the tire pressure even though the tires are warm.

J However, if you have radial tires, you usually cannot tell by looking at them if they are underinflated.

3 You can check the air pressure even on a "warm tire." If the pressure seems too low, increase it to the recommended "cold" level. Your tire may still be underinflated because the warm air in it makes the pressure level temporarily higher. _____ Don't forget to check the air pressure again when the tire is cold.

A Use your tire gauge to check the air pressure.

B You must use a gas station air pump to increase the pressure.

C However, it's better to drive with slightly low air pressure than with really low pressure.

D Wait until the car has not been driven for several hours before rechecking the pressure.

4 Safe tires have enough tread to grip wet and icy roads. Tires should be replaced when their tread is worn down to $\frac{1}{16}$ inch. Many tires have built-in indicators to tell you when the tread is too low. Another method is to place a penny in the tread. _____ If you can see the top of his head, the tread is too low.

F Tire treads provide traction.

G Check your tire treads frequently.

H The indicators are in the bottom of the tread grooves.

J Make sure Abraham Lincoln's head is upside down and facing you.

Check your answers on pages 91–92.

Lesson 21 Connective and Transition Words

Connective words and phrases such as *however, in addition,* and *as a result* help link ideas in writing. The TABE will ask you to read a paragraph and choose a sentence that begins with the correct connective word. First you must decide how the sentence is related to the other ideas in the paragraph. Does it *contradict* another idea? Is it an *example* of another idea? Is it the *result* of another idea? The answers to these questions will tell you which connective word is correct.

Example **Read the paragraph. Then choose a connective word from the box to fill in the blank in the last sentence.**

If you have e-mail, you are sure to receive messages about opportunities to work at home and earn huge amounts of money. The offers are very tempting. _____, they are almost always misleading.

Meaning	Connective Word
addition or comparison	besides, similarly
contradiction	nevertheless, however, on the other hand
defiance	in spite of this
result	consequently, therefore, as a result
time	finally
example	for example

Did you choose a word from the "contradiction" group? *Nevertheless* or *however,* for example, would correctly show that the last sentence contradicts the sentence before it.

Test Example

Read the paragraph. Then choose the sentence that best fills the blank in the paragraph.

1   Internet scams often target parents who stay home with their children. These scams promise an opportunity to balance the demands of work and home. _____

A   For example, one scam promises that an investment of $10 will lead to earnings of $40,000.

B   Nevertheless, one scam promises that an investment of $10 will lead to earnings of $40,000.

C   As a result, one scam promises that an investment of $10 will lead to earnings of $40,000.

D   Besides, one scam promises that an investment of $10 will lead to earnings of $40,000.

Hint

First decide how the missing sentence relates to the other sentences in the paragraph.

1 **A** This sentence describes an example of a scam. The other options are incorrect. Option B suggests that the scam contradicts the previous sentence. Option C suggests that the scam is caused by the previous sentence. Option D suggests that the scam is in addition to something in the previous sentence.

Practice

Read the paragraphs. Then choose the sentence that best fills the blank in each paragraph.

1 Don't rely on a respected Web site to warn you of scams. You can find some scams at Web sites that are usually trustworthy. These "business opportunities" look so safe. _____ In the same way, some respected magazines and newspapers do not evaluate the products they advertise.

A However, many Web sites do not check out their advertisers.

B Similarly, many Web sites do not check out their advertisers.

C Consequently, many Web sites do not check out their advertisers.

D In spite of this, many Web sites do not check out their advertisers.

2 Get-rich schemes are nothing new. They have existed since the first business was formed. Now, however, the Internet allows us to communicate with one another much more easily. It has become a major way for us to do business. _____

F Besides, scam artists use the Internet to find their targets.

G Nevertheless, scam artists now use the Internet to find their targets.

H Finally, scam artists are beginning to use the Internet to find their targets.

J As a result, it has become a favorite way for scam artists to find their targets.

3 Some job ads list real requirements, such as skill in software development, bookkeeping, or accounting. These ads, along with those looking for telemarketers, are more likely to be legitimate. _____

A In spite of this, you are probably safe in replying to them.

B Therefore, you are probably safe in replying to them.

C Similarly, you are probably safe in replying to them.

D Finally, you are probably safe in replying to them.

Check your answers on page 92.

A paragraph should begin with a strong topic sentence, followed by supporting sentences. However, each supporting sentence must be closely related to the topic and not go off in another direction. The TABE will ask you to read a paragraph and choose the sentence that does not belong: the unrelated sentence. This lesson will help you learn to determine which sentence is unrelated.

Example **Read the paragraph. Which sentence does <u>not</u> belong in the paragraph?**

The sentences are numbered to identify them. _____

1. Do you pack a school lunch for your child every morning? 2. You want to pack a nutritious, well-balanced lunch that your child will want to eat, not trade or toss in the trash. 3. Children's tastes often change from one week to the next. 4. To pack a tempting lunch, all you need is some planning, your imagination, and a little communication with your child.

Sentence 3 does not belong because the paragraph is about packing school lunches, not children's changing tastes. Sentences 1, 2, and 4 stay on the topic of packing lunches.

Test Example

Read the paragraph. Then choose the sentence that does <u>not</u> belong in the paragraph.

1 1. Begin by asking your child what he or she wants for lunch during the coming week. 2. Then make your own weekly school lunch menu, and take the menu with you when you go grocery shopping. 3. That way, you will have the ingredients you need on hand every morning. 4. Mornings can be a time of confusion and rushing around.

  A Sentence 1

  B Sentence 2

  C Sentence 3

  D Sentence 4

TABE Strategy

Read all the sentences before deciding which one is slightly off the topic.

1 **D** The paragraph is about planning for school lunches, not the morning rush. Options A, B, and C are about planning school lunches and belong in the paragraph.

Read each paragraph. Then choose the sentence that does <u>not</u> belong in the paragraph.

1
1. As you pack school lunches, you don't have to stick to plain white bread. 2. You can experiment with bagels, pita pockets, English muffins, and whole-grain or multigrain breads. 3. Bread is an important part of the Food Guide Pyramid. 4. You can also cut the bread into fun shapes to surprise your son or daughter.

A Sentence 1

B Sentence 2

C Sentence 3

D Sentence 4

2
1. Does your child like raw vegetables? 2. As you know, vegetables contain many essential vitamins. 3. Even a fussy child will eat vegetables if they are presented in an interesting way. 4. For example, try making a crunchy caterpillar out of carrot and zucchini rounds, alternating them on a toothpick.

F Sentence 1

G Sentence 2

H Sentence 3

J Sentence 4

3
1. Don't miss this opportunity to communicate with your child. 2. Occasionally pack a note with your child's lunch, saying how much you love your son or daughter and how proud you are of him or her. 3. You might also wish your child good luck on a test or on the tryouts for the band, a play, or a sports team. 4. Tryouts can be a stressful time for any child.

A Sentence 1

B Sentence 2

C Sentence 3

D Sentence 4

4
1. Remember to protect your child from food poisoning. 2. Pack the lunch so that cold things stay cold and hot things stay hot. 3. The lunch should be simple and neat to eat. 4. An insulated lunch container or refreezable ice packs can help.

F Sentence 1

G Sentence 2

H Sentence 3

J Sentence 4

Check your answers on page 92.

For numbers 1 and 2, read the paragraph. Then choose the sentence that best fills the blank in the paragraph.

1 _____ The doctors use a three-armed robot. It can make the same movements as the surgeon. However, the surgeon is hundreds of miles away in another hospital.

   A Robots are becoming more useful every day.

   B Most surgery used to involve large incisions that healed slowly.

   C Doctors are always trying to improve their surgical techniques.

   D Two surgeons are now performing operations by remote control.

2 The operations performed in this way do not require large incisions. Instead, the surgery is completed through a small incision. It does not require a long healing period. _____

   F However, patients are up and back home in two days or less.

   G As a result, patients are up and back home in two days or less.

   H Similarly, the surgical instruments are inserted through this incision.

   J Nevertheless, the surgical instruments are inserted through this incision.

For number 3, choose the answer that best develops this topic sentence.

3 This technique is called hospital-to-hospital telerobotics-assisted surgery.

   A Many small hospitals cannot afford to keep highly trained surgeons on hand. They often must send patients to other hospitals that can meet their needs.

   B In one hospital, a skilled surgeon slips his hands around computer controls. In a hospital far away, a robot imitates the movements of the doctor's hands.

   C Robots are often used in manufacturing. They can perform precise movements that are difficult for human workers.

   D The surgeons using this technique are based in Canada. The robot is named Zeus.

For number 4, read the paragraph. Then choose the sentence that does <u>not</u> belong in the paragraph.

4 1. Dr. Mehran Anvari was one of the first to perform this new kind of surgery. 2. It may transform surgery much as the Industrial Revolution transformed manufacturing. 3. Dr. Anvari now spends much of his time teaching others. 4. All patients prefer to have small incisions because of the shorter healing time.

   F Sentence 1   **H** Sentence 3

   G Sentence 2   **J** Sentence 4

Check your answers on page 92.

Lesson 23 Capitalization

Many words should begin with capital letters. For example, the first word of a sentence begins with a capital letter. The names of months and the days of the week also begin with capital letters. The table below categorizes different kinds of words that should begin with capital letters.

Kind of Word	Examples
first word of sentence	The early bird gets the worm.
months	January, February, March
days of the week	Monday, Tuesday, Wednesday
names of publications, works of art	*The Daily Herald,* "Mona Lisa"
specific streets, buildings, places, and geographical locations	Main Street, Sears Tower, Central Park, Kansas City

Example **Read the sentence. Circle the words that should be capitalized and underline the word that should not be capitalized.**

next summer I will Volunteer at turkey run State Park.

Did you circle *Next* and *Turkey Run*? Did you underline *Volunteer*? *Next* is the first word of the sentence. *Turkey Run State Park* is the name of a place, so all of the words should be capitalized. *Volunteer* is a verb and should not be capitalized.

Hint

Do not capitalize the names of the seasons (spring, summer, autumn, winter).

Test Example

Choose the sentence that is written correctly and shows the correct capitalization.

1 A The Benefits of volunteering vary with the experience.

  B Last october, Kira signed up to be a community volunteer.

  C Volunteering at Children's Riverside Park allowed her to gain new skills.

  D Volunteering at any Park could help you gain new skills, too.

1   C The first word and the specific name of the park, *Children's Riverside Park*, need capital letters. In option A, *Benefits* is incorrectly capitalized. In option B, the month, *October*, should be capitalized. Option D names a park, generally, but it is not the name of a specific park and, therefore, should not be capitalized.

Practice

For numbers 1 and 2, read the paragraph. Look at the numbered, underlined portions. Choose the answer that is written correctly for each underlined portion.

(1)　　　Anybody can help make a place <u>better. helping</u> does not require a college degree or years of experience. For example, the staff at the

(2)　<u>Owen National Forest</u> are always looking for volunteers. There are jobs for people of all ages and abilities.

1　A better. Helping

　　B Better helping

　　C Better. helping

　　D Correct as it is

2　F owen national forest

　　G Owen national forest

　　H Owen National forest

　　J Correct as it is

For numbers 3 through 5, choose the sentence that is written correctly and shows the correct capitalization.

3　A Everyone agrees that the White River needs a clean-up.

　　B More than 60 Citizens showed up to help.

　　C We agreed to work every saturday in April.

　　D The flooding that occurred in february really made a mess of the banks.

4　F The River also passes through Indianapolis.

　　G workers of all kinds stroll along the banks at lunchtime.

　　H Most people in the City know how beautiful it is there in summer.

　　J There's a nice poem, titled "Along the River," that tells about it.

5　A Our School is going to help clean up the river.

　　B The river passes through the Western edge of town.

　　C Cooper Park lies right along the River, too.

　　D The whole community will turn out for a celebration in June!

Check your answers on page 92.

Lesson 24 End Marks

Every sentence must have an end mark. A statement should end with a period, and a question should end with a question mark. A sentence expressing strong emotion should end with an exclamation point. The chart below will help you brush up on end marks so you can use them correctly in your writing and on the TABE.

Period	Sentences that are a statement or command end with a period. *I am planning to take an important test.*
Question mark	Sentences that ask a question end with a question mark. *How do you think you will do on the test?*
Exclamation point	Sentences that show emotion, surprise, or strong feelings end with an exclamation point. *I did great on the test!*

Example Read the two sentences and write the correct end marks on the lines at the end of the sentences.

Sentence A How can young adults become healthier _____

Sentence B A healthful diet is not the whole answer _____

Did you add a question mark to Sentence A and a period to Sentence B? Using any other end marks for this question and this statement would be incorrect.

Test Example

Read the sentence and look at the underlined portion. Choose the answer that is written correctly for that underlined portion.

Physical activity can benefit people of nearly any age, this activity does not have to be strenuous to be beneficial, however.

1 A age this

   B age! This

   C age. This

   D Correct as it is

Hint

How can you tell a statement from an exclamation? Look for strong feelings.

1 C The word *age* ends a statement, so it should be followed by a period. The word *this* begins a new sentence and should be capitalized. Option A creates a run-on sentence. The first sentence does not express a strong emotion, so an exclamation point (option B) is incorrect. The sentences are not correct as they are (option D) because they should not be separated with a comma.

For numbers 1 through 3, read the paragraph. Look at the numbered, underlined portions. Choose the answer that is written correctly for each underlined portion.

Did you know that nearly half of young Americans do not engage in physical
(1) activity on a regular basis! In fact, young people tend to become less active as they
(2) get older? This situation absolutely has to
(3) change?

1

A basis; in

B basis. In

C basis? In

D Correct as it is

2

F older this

G older, this

H older. This

J Correct as it is

3

A change.

B change!

C change,

D Correct as it is

For numbers 4 through 6, decide which punctuation mark, if any, is needed in the sentence.

4 What can communities do to help

F .   G !   H ?   J None

5 First, schools can make sure that physical education classes are available

A .   B ,   C ?   D None

6 We must wake up to this growing problem that is posing great danger

F ,   G !   H ?   J None

Check your answers on page 92.

Commas and Semicolons

The comma is the most used punctuation mark. It has more uses and rules than any other punctuation mark. It is used as a separator. It marks a pause in a sentence. A semicolon is a stronger punctuation mark. It is stronger than the brief pause of a comma, but not as strong as the full stop of a period. It tells readers that the two complete sentences it separates are related and need to stay connected. The most common uses of commas and semicolons are in the table below.

Uses of Commas
Names   Commas are used to set off the names of people to whom you are talking.   • Jeff, did you see my book?
Introductory Words and Phrases   Commas are used to set off certain words and phrases at the beginning of sentences.   • Without a doubt, I haven't seen it.   • If she doesn't answer the door, ring the doorbell again.
Words That Rename   Commas are used to set off the words that rename something.   • I read that in *The Times,* our local newspaper.
City and State   Commas are used to separate a city from a state.   • My cousin lives in Tempe, Arizona.

Use of Semicolons
Related Sentences   Semicolons are used to separate complete sentences that depend on each other for meaning.   • The diner is open daily; its food is the best around.

Example **Read the sentences. Which sentence uses commas correctly?** _____

> **Sentence A** If she doesn't return your call, try calling again later.
> **Sentence B** Unfortunately getting hired is only the first challenge in a new job.

Sentence A uses commas correctly. Sentence B is not correct because there should be a comma after the introductory word *Unfortunately*.

Test Example

Choose the sentence that is written correctly.

1 A Without a doubt making a good first impression on a new boss is important.

   B In fact, a good first impression can make your first weeks go smoothly.

   C Keith my brother recently started a new job at a local company.

   D He just moved back here from, Jackson Wyoming.

Practice

For numbers 1 through 4, read the paragraph. Look at the numbered, underlined portions. Choose the answer that is written correctly for each underlined portion.

(1)   John Hershey, Keith's new manager asked Keith to be at work by 8:00 a.m. My brother arrived at 7:30 the first day.
(2)   After that he started sleeping in. I warned him that a good first
(3)   impression does not last forever however Keith just smiled and
(4)   left for work, late again. Before long, Keith had lost his job.

1
A Hershey. Keith's new manager
B Hershey; Keith's new manager
C Hershey, Keith's new manager,
D Correct as it is

2
F After that, he started
G After, that he started
H After that he started,
J Correct as it is

3
A forever; however
B forever, however,
C forever; however,
D Correct as it is

4
F Before, long
G Before long
H Before long;
J Correct as it is

For number 5, choose the sentence that is written correctly.

5
A Still making a first impression is not difficult.
B Whatever you do, do not try to cover up your mistakes.
C If you listen carefully you will not need to ask as many questions.
D At the same time be sure to ask about anything that you do not understand.

For number 6, decide which punctuation mark, if any, is needed in the sentence.

6   Keith what time are you supposed to be at your new job?
F ;   G .   H ,   J None

Check your answers on pages 92–93.

For numbers 1 through 4, read the paragraph. Look at the numbered, underlined portions. Choose the answer that is written correctly for each underlined portion.

 Suppose you are offered a job you interviewed for and then

(1) decide you do not want <u>it what</u> should you do? You still must write

(2) a thank-you note to Ms. <u>Baker, the</u> person who interviewed you. You can use your note to explain why the job is not a good fit for

(3) <u>you in fact</u> you can even mention another job that would interest

(4) you if it becomes available. <u>writing a thank-you note</u> shows that you have good manners and business etiquette and that you are organized.

1
  A it, what
  B it. What
  C it? What
  D Correct as it is

2
  F Baker the
  G Baker; the
  H Baker. The
  J Correct as it is

3
  A you; in fact
  B you, in fact
  C you; in fact,
  D Correct as it is

4
  F writing a Thank-You note
  G Writing a thank-you note
  H Writing a Thank-You Note
  J Correct as it is

For numbers 5 and 6, choose the sentence that is written correctly and shows the correct capitalization and punctuation.

5
  A Above all, be respectful of the interviewer's time.
  B This Company might have another job opening soon.
  C Corey didn't you have a job interview sometime last Month?
  D No I had an interview in february but the pay was not high enough.

6
  F Some experts recommend that you dress like your Boss.
  G Always be on time for work even if you don't have to punch into a Time Clock.
  H Keep your career goals in mind and keep working toward them.
  J Don't stick with a job if it's not right, for you.

Check your answers on page 93.

Lesson 26 Quotation Marks

Quotation marks come in pairs. They are used to enclose quotations, the exact words that people speak. The box below lists rules for using quotation marks.

Rules for Using Quotation Marks

- When the direct quotation is a complete sentence, it begins with a capital letter and ends with a period.
    Art said, "**I** really need a new job."
- When the quotation is a sentence fragment, it does not begin with a capital letter.
    Art said his last job was "**t**he best ever."
- Use a comma after phrases such as *Art said* when they come before the quotation.
    Art said**,** "Give me the classified ads."
- Use a comma followed by a quotation mark after the last word of a quotation when it is followed by a phrase.
    "It's time to go to the job interview**,"** Art said.
- Question marks and exclamation points are placed inside the ending quotation mark when they are part of the quotation.
    Tom asked, "Are you prepared for your interview**?"**
- Question marks and exclamation points are placed outside the ending quotation mark when they are not part of the quotation.
    Were you surprised when the interviewer said, "I'd love to have you back for a second interview"**?**

Example Read the sentence. What is missing? _____

Art said, "Yesterday I heard that the factory on Canal Street is hiring.

The ending quotation mark is missing. The speaker's words start with a quotation mark and are set off from *Art said* with a comma. The quotation also begins with a capital letter on *Yesterday* and ends with a period. Only the ending quotation mark needs to be added.

Test Example

Read the sentence and look at the underlined portion. Choose the answer that is written correctly for that underlined portion.

"Do you mean Carter <u>Manufacturing" I</u> asked Art.

1 A Manufacturing." I

   B Manufacturing," I

   C Manufacturing?" I

   D Correct as it is

Hint
Decide what kind of sentence the quotation is before you choose an end mark.

1 C This quotation is a question, so it should end with a question mark. The period in option A is incorrect, as it divides the words into two sentences. The comma in option B would be correct if the quotation were a statement. As written (option D), the sentence is incorrect because it needs a question mark.

Practice

For numbers 1 and 2, read the passage. Look at the numbered, underlined portions. Choose the answer that is written correctly for each underlined portion.

(1) "I think Carter Manufacturing has some jobs open on the third <u>shift, I</u> told Art.
(2) "I wouldn't mind working at night," Art <u>said. "sleeping</u> during the day is usually not a problem for me."

1
A shift. I
B shift," I
C shift?" I
D Correct as it is

2
F said. Sleeping
G said. "Sleeping
H said, "Sleeping
J Correct as it is

For numbers 3 and 4, decide which punctuation mark, if any, is needed in the sentence.

3 "I think," Art told me, "that I'll go down to Carter and put in an application"

A .   C ?
B ,   D None

4 I said "If you wait a minute, I'll come with you and put an application in, too."

F .   H ?
G ,   J None

For numbers 5 and 6, choose the sentence that is correctly written.

5
A "Do you think we will need a resume? I asked.
B "No," Art said. "those folks have a form to fill out."
C "I think you must have applied at Carter before," I said.
D He nodded and said, "I applied there about a year or two ago.

6
F Art checked his wallet and said "I think I left my Social Security card at home."
G "Can't you just write your number on the application." I asked him.
H Art shook his head and said, "I can never remember what it is."
J He shrugged and said, "it starts with either 285 or 258."

Check your answers on page 93.

Apostrophes have two main uses in writing. They are used to show ownership, and they are used in contractions such as *it's*, a combination of "it is." The box below details some rules for using apostrophes.

Using Apostrophes to Show Ownership

- When the noun is singular, you usually add *'s* (cat's).
- When the noun is plural and already ends in *s*, you just add an apostrophe (cats').

Using Apostrophes in Contractions

- Apostrophes are used in contractions to show that one or more letters are missing.
- One of the trickiest contractions is *it's*, a contraction of "it is." "It's getting dark earlier now" means "It is getting dark earlier now."
- *Its* without the apostrophe is <u>not</u> a contraction. *Its* shows possession: "The tree lost its leaves." It would <u>not</u> make sense to say, "The tree lost it is leaves."
- If you are confused about whether a word is the possessive *its* or the contraction *it's*, speak the sentence aloud using *it is* in place of *it's* or *its*. If it makes sense using *it is*, then it is a contraction and should have an apostrophe. If it doesn't make sense, then it is possessive and does not need an apostrophe. "*It's* time to go to school" means "*It is* time to go to school."

Example Read the sentence. There are two missing apostrophes. Where should they go? _____

Its time to bake Lindas birthday cake.

An apostrophe should be inserted before the *s* in *Its* and *Lindas*. *It's* is a contraction of *it is*, and *Linda's* is a singular possessive noun.

Test Example

Read the sentence and look at the underlined portion. Choose the answer that is written correctly for that underlined portion.

Suddenly <u>its</u> January and time to list the things you want to change about your life.

1 A its'

    B it's

    C it was

    D Correct as it is

TABE Strategy

If you have time left at the end of the test, go back and check your answers. Make sure you have filled in every bubble on the answer sheet.

1 **B** This word is a contraction of *it is*, so it requires an apostrophe. In option A, the apostrophe is in the wrong place. In option C, the tense is changed, making the sentence confusing. In option D, the possessive form of *its* is incorrectly used.

For numbers 1 through 3, read the paragraph. Look at the numbered, underlined portions. Choose the answer that is written correctly for each underlined portion.

(1)   As the new year begins, it's easy to find people who are making their <u>resolutions</u>. For example, my
(2)   <u>friends</u> brother just made his resolution. He wants to save enough money to buy a new car because his
(3)   old one is on <u>it's</u> way to the junkyard.

1 A its
    B its'
    C it will be
    D Correct as it is

2 F friend
    G friends'
    H friend's
    J Correct as it is

3 A its
    B its'
    C it is
    D Correct as it is

For numbers 4 through 6, choose the sentence that is correctly written.

4 F People often break their resolutions because their goals' are unreasonable.
    G My neighbors resolution was to lose 30 pounds in two months.
    H It's clear to everyone but him that he cannot do that safely.
    J For everything he eats, he wants to know it's calories.

5 A Experts recommend that peoples goals be important to them.
    B Its not going to work if someone chooses your goals for you.
    C You need to set a goal because it's what you want to do.
    D A friends' goal may not be the right one for you.

6 F Before you choose a goal, make sure it's a priority in your life.
    G If its important to you, you will work to reach it.
    H Experts suggestions can offer some guidance.
    J Still, your own priorities' are what counts.

Check your answers on page 93.

Do you know how to punctuate a business letter? Here are some important rules to remember:

Dates
Use a comma after the day.
June 10, 2004
Addresses
Capitalize abbreviations and end them with a period.
Use a comma to separate the city and the state.
247 Harbor Bridge Dr.
Wilmington, Delaware 19880
Greeting or Salutation
Use a colon in a business letter.
Dear Mr. Stevens:
Closing
Capitalize only the first word and end with a comma.
Yours truly,

Example **Read the address. List two punctuation errors.** _____

_____

79 Green Hill St
St. Louis Missouri, 63103

There should be a period after *St* and a comma after *St. Louis* instead of after *Missouri*. Abbreviations such as *St.* should end with a period. The comma goes after the city, not after the state.

Test Example

Read the letter closing. Choose the answer that shows the correct form for a closing.

1   Best regards

   A   best regards,

   B   Best Regards

   C   Best regards,

   D   Correct as it is

1   C   In option C, the first word is capitalized and the closing ends with a comma. In option A, *best* should be capitalized. In option B, *Regards* should not be capitalized, and a comma should be added. This closing is not correct as written (option D), as it should end with a comma.

Read the letter. Look at the numbered, underlined portions. Choose the answer that is written correctly for each underlined portion.

---

(1) <u>May 13, 2004</u>

Harriet Conners
Third Shift Supervisor
Carter Manufacturing
(2) <u>18 Canal st.</u>
(3) <u>Denver Colorado 80209</u>

(4) <u>Dear Ms. Conners,</u>

Thank you for talking with me at my interview last Friday. My friends have told me for years that Carter is an excellent place to work, and I am sure now that they are correct.

If I can answer any questions or provide any information that will help convince you to hire me, I'll do it gladly. I look forward to hearing from you.

(5) <u>Sincerely Yours,</u>

Art Rosswell

Art Rosswell

1
A May 13 2004
B May 13 2004,
C may 13, 2004
D Correct as it is

2
F 18 Canal st
G 18 Canal St
H 18 Canal St.
J Correct as it is

3
A Denver, Colorado 80209
B Denver Colorado, 80209
C Denver, Colorado, 80209
D Correct as it is

4
F Dear Harriet,
G Dear Ms. Conners
H Dear Ms. Conners:
J Correct as it is

5
A sincerely yours:
B Sincerely Yours
C Sincerely yours,
D Correct as it is

Check your answers on page 94.

Read the letter. Look at the numbered, underlined portions. Choose the answer that is written correctly for each underlined portion.

(1) August, 4 2004

Benjamin Means, Manager
Ajax Foods
(2) 274 Benson Ave
Lawrence, Kansas 66046

Dear Mr. Means:

I really appreciate your job offer, and I look forward to starting at Ajax Foods on September 1. When I told my neighbor about my
(3) new job, she said "Max, you're a lucky man to work for that
(4) company." I am sure that she is right.
(5) My neighbors name, by the way, is Patty Thomas, and she says she knows you! She tells me that you worked together in the marketing department of the Food Corporation ten years ago.
(6) I am glad to be part of Ajax because of its excellent reputation.

Yours Truly,

Max Garcia

Max Garcia

1 **A** August 4 2004
   B august 4, 2004
   C August 4, 2004
   D Correct as it is

2 **F** 274 Benson ave
   G 274 Benson ave.
   H 274 Benson Ave.
   J Correct as it is

3 **A** said Max,
   B said. "Max,
   C said, "Max,
   D Correct as it is

4 **F** company.
   G company"
   H company,"
   J Correct as it is

5 **A** neighbors'
   B neighbor's
   C neighbors's
   D Correct as it is

6 **F** its'
   G it's
   H it is
   J Correct as it is

Check your answers on page 94.

Lesson 29 Vowels

The vowels—*a, e, i, o, u,* and sometimes *y*—can be used to represent many spoken sounds. With some practice, you will know how to spell the vowel sound in every word. The TABE will test you on four kinds of vowels. Those four types of vowels are explained in this lesson.

Examples **Read the sentences. Then circle the word that is spelled correctly and best completes each sentence.**

Which workers were selected as the union _____? (delegates   delugates)

The correct spelling is *delegates*. The other option is misspelled. This is an example of a **short vowel**. A short vowel sound cannot come at the end of a word.

Our community is trying to _____ water during the drought.

(consorve   conserve)

The correct spelling is *conserve*. The other option is misspelled. This is an example of an **r-controlled vowel**. When the letter *r* follows a vowel, the vowel usually changes its sound. For example, compare *bat* and *bar*, *fat* and *far*, or *sit* and *sir*.

I will write him a letter with my _____. (apology   apolugy)

The correct spelling is *apology*. The other option is misspelled. This is an example of a **schwa** vowel. This vowel sound sounds like "uh." Speak the word aloud slowly, and you will hear the "uh" as the third syllable. The schwa is often spelled with an *a*, but can also be spelled with an *e, i,* or *o*. Some other examples of the schwa vowel sound include the third syllable in *temperature* and the second syllable in *amateur*.

Test Example

Choose the word that is spelled correctly and best completes the sentence.

1 Working parents do not have much time for _____.

A leesure   C leisure

B liesure   D leasure

Hint

The spelling of some words does not follow the rules. It just has to be memorized.

1 **C** The correct spelling is *leisure*. The other options are misspelled. This is an example of a **long vowel**. The first vowel in *leisure* is a long *e* sound. In general, long vowels are pronounced like the name of the letter. Some long vowel sounds, like this one, are spelled with a combination of letters. You might have learned to use *i* before *e* except after *c*. However, there are always exceptions to the rules, and this is one of them.

Lesson 30 Consonants

There are 21 consonant letters in the alphabet. Consonants are all the letters except the vowels *a, e, i, o,* and *u.* Consonants can be tricky. Sometimes they are doubled, and sometimes they are spelled differently from the sound they make. In addition, different letters can represent the same consonant sound, as you can see from the chart below.

Sound	Different Spellings
s sound	s (street), c (circus), sc (miscellaneous)
sh sound	ti (substantial), ci (financial)
j sound	j (junior), g (mortgage)
f sound	f (farmers), ph (pamphlet)

Examples **Read the sentences. Choose the word that is spelled correctly and best completes each sentence.**

He was known as a _____ worker. (consciencous   conscientious)

The correct spelling is *conscientious*. The other option is misspelled. This is an example of a **variant spelling.** Many words are spelled with one consonant, but pronounced with a different consonant sound. The *sh* sound can be spelled several ways, and in *conscientious,* it is spelled *ti.*

The _____ for our meeting were luxurious.

(accommodations   acomodations)

The correct spelling is *accommodations*. The other option is misspelled. This is an example of a **double letter consonant.** Doubling a consonant does not change the way the word is pronounced. *Accommodations* has a double *c* and a double *m.*

June says her new job sounds _____. (fascinating   fasenateing)

The correct spelling is *fascinating*. The other option is misspelled. This is an example of a **silent letter.** The *c* in *fascinating* is silent. To correctly spell words that have silent consonants, you have to include the consonants. *Fascinate* also ends with a silent *e,* which must be dropped before adding *-ing*: *fascinat+ing.*

Test Example

Choose the word that is spelled correctly and best completes the sentence.

1 Did you turn in your _____ yet?

   A resegnnation   C resignation

   B rezegnation   D rezignation

Hint

Don't be fooled by a spelling that sounds correct when you say it aloud. It may still be incorrect.

1 C The correct spelling is *resignation*. The other options are misspelled. This is a variant spelling. The second consonant sounds like a *z* but is pronounced like an *s.*

It can be easier to spell a word if you break it into parts. It helps to look for the root, or main part, of the word, and also any prefixes or suffixes. It also helps to memorize difficult word spellings.

Examples Read the sentences. Circle the word that is spelled correctly and best completes each sentence.

Maria has always been a _____ manager.

(competent   competant)

The correct spelling is *competent*. Endings like -ance, -ence, -ant, and -ent are easy to confuse because there is no clear clue to the spelling. You can get clues from **similar words**. For example, the last syllable of *competent* sounds like the last syllable of *insistent*. If you know that *insistent* is spelled with an *e* in the last syllable, then you can make an educated guess that *competent* is also spelled with an *e* in the last syllable.

A weather _____ shows which way the wind is blowing. (vein   vane)

The correct spelling is *vane*. A *vane* shows wind direction. A *vein*, on the other hand, is a blood vessel. This kind of word is called a **homonym**. Homonyms are two or more words that have different meanings that are spelled differently but pronounced exactly the same.

Moving to a new office was more _____ than I expected.

(strenuose   strenuous)

The correct spelling is *strenuous*. The key to spelling this word is knowing how to spell the **suffix**, the ending of the word. The suffix of *strenuous* is *ous*. It sounds like *us*, but it is spelled *ous*.

Is your computer _____ with the new software?

(eqwipped   equipped)

The correct spelling is *equipped*. The key to spelling this word is knowing how to spell the **root**, the word on which the word is based. The root of *equipped* is *equip*. *Equip* is a two-syllable word that ends with one consonant. When you say *equip*, the last syllable is louder than the first. For words like *equip*, you double the last consonant before adding the ending: *equip+p+ed*.

Test Example

Choose the word that is spelled correctly and best completes the sentence.

1 I checked the _____ of parts in the warehouse.

   A quanities   C quantites

   B quantitys   D quanties

Hint

More than one answer may be spelled correctly. Choose the option that best completes the sentence.

1 D *Quantity* ends in *y*, which is changed to *i* before adding the ending: *quantit+i+es*. To decide how to spell this word, think about the spelling of similar word parts, like *qualities* or *identities*.

Choose the word that is spelled correctly and best completes the sentence.

1 His _____ at work has been excellent.

    A attendence

    B attendance

    C attendents

    D attendants

2 Ms. Jeffery will be the company's new _____.

    F treassurer

    G treasurer

    H tressurer

    J tresurer

3 Everyone signed the _____ for a four-day workweek.

    A putition

    B petition

    C patition

    D pitition

4 Our salespeople are _____ to everyone.

    F curteous

    G curtious

    H courtious

    J courteous

5 My promotion begins on the _____ of May.

    A twelveth

    B twelvth

    C twelfth

    D twelth

6 You just need to add your _____ to the contract.

    F signiture

    G signeture

    H signature

    J signoture

7 The summer workers threatened to have a _____.

    A rebellion

    B rebellon

    C rebelion

    D rebelon

8 What rate does that bank offer for a _____?

    F morgaje

    G morgage

    H mortgaje

    J mortgage

9 Our company has been in _____ for thirty years.

    A exsistence

    B existence

    C existance

    D existince

10 The company cafeteria serves three kinds of _____.

    F serial

    G ceriel

    H seriel

    J cereal

11 I have always wanted to live a life of _____.

  A liesure

  B leesure

  C leisure

  D leasure

12 My workout was _____.

  F strenuos

  G strenous

  H strenuous

  J strenuose

13 Our weather _____ has stood up to the wind for years.

  A vein

  B vane

  C vain

  D veine

14 Jermaine is highly _____ at his job.

  F compitant

  G compitent

  H competent

  J competant

15 She dedicates a _____ amount of her free time to volunteering.

  A substanciul

  B substantiul

  C substantial

  D substancial

16 Find out if you are _____ for financial aid.

  F eligible

  G eligeble

  H eliguble

  J eligable

17 I am meeting with the admissions counselor at the _____.

  A university

  B unaversity

  C unoversity

  D uneversity

18 I save money by buying in large _____.

  F quintities

  G quantities

  H quontities

  J kwantities

19 It is always a good idea to _____ natural resources.

  A consirve

  B consurve

  C conserve

  D conserv

20 The story was _____.

  F fasenating

  G fassinating

  H fassenating

  J fascinating

Check your answers on page 94.

The Language Performance Assessment is identical to the real TABE in format and length. It will give you an idea of what the actual test is like. Allow yourself 39 minutes to complete this assessment. Check your answers on pages 95–97.

Sample A

A   The Manufacturing Plant is about 12 miles from my apartment.

B   The problem of getting through the rush hour traffic.

C   An accident on Route 3 made me late for work.

D   Every morning, I get to work regularly on time.

Sample B

The shirts had the company's name on them.

The shirts were blue.

F   The shirts had the company's blue name on them.

G   The blue shirts had the company's name on them.

H   The shirts had the company's name on them, and they were blue.

J   The shirts had the company's name on them, and the shirts were blue.

Sample C

Has she seen the new schedule. i saw it this morning.

A   schedule. I

B   schedule, I

C   schedule? I

D   Correct as it is

Sample D

F   I have a note from Mr. Bernard.

G   Did you go shopping.

H   Please hand me an apple

J   Can we go to the market wednesday?

Page 75

Go On ▶

For numbers 1 through 3, decide which punctuation mark, if any, is needed in each sentence.

1   Evan did that package go out in today's mail?

    A .   **B** ,   **C** "   **D** None

2   I will have it ready first thing tomorrow morning

    F .   **G** ,   **H** ?   **J** None

3   "Did you include the box of valves in that package? asked George.

    A .   **B** !   **C** "   **D** None

For numbers 4 through 7, read the underlined sentences. Then choose the sentence that best combines those sentences into one.

4   The plant hired a new supervisor for its assembly lines.

    The supervisor is from Chicago.

    F The plant hired a new supervisor for its assembly lines from Chicago.

    G The plant from Chicago hired a new supervisor for its assembly lines.

    H The plant hired a new supervisor from Chicago for its assembly lines.

    J The plant hired a new supervisor for its assembly lines, and he is from Chicago.

5   The wind was swirling around the buildings in the deserted town.

    The buildings were old and battered.

    A The wind was swirling around the buildings in the deserted town, and the buildings were old and battered.

    B The wind was swirling around the old, battered buildings in the deserted town.

    C The old, battered wind was swirling around the buildings in the deserted town.

    D The wind was swirling around the buildings in the battered, deserted old town.

6 Julia just got a promotion to senior technician.

Hank was also promoted to senior technician.

F Julia and Hank were just promoted to senior technician.

G Julia was promoted and Hank was promoted to senior technician.

H Julia just got a promotion to senior technician, and Hank was also promoted.

J Julia just got a promotion to senior technician, and Hank got the same promotion.

7 The automotive plant in Middletown just opened a new building.

The plant will probably be hiring more workers.

A The automotive plant in Middletown just opened a new building, or the plant will probably be hiring more workers.

B The automotive plant in Middletown just opened a new building, so the plant will probably be hiring more workers.

C The automotive plant in Middletown just opened a new building because it hired more workers.

D Being in Middletown, the new building at the automotive plant probably will hire more workers.

For numbers 8 through 18, choose the sentence that is written correctly and shows the correct capitalization and punctuation. Be sure the sentence you choose is complete.

8 **F** The company's headquarters is at the corner of Oak Street and High.

G I have an interview scheduled with Ms. Henderson on march 14.

H That day is also my Birthday, which I think is good luck.

J The Company started hiring people last Month.

9 **A** Walking through the door, the television blared the news.

B I stopped my bike, took off my hat, and locked it to the rack.

C After eating breakfast, the commuter van beeped its horn.

D Knowing that I was late, I rushed into the office all out of breath.

10 **F** I work every day of the week accept Friday.

G Last year, our union excepted a four-day workweek.

H Not everyone wanted to accept working four longer days.

J Now most people are happy with a shorter week, accept on Monday mornings.

11 **A** For vacation this Summer, we are headed for the Outer Banks in North Carolina.

B Our family gets together and rents the same house there every year.

C It's on the Southern tip of the Outer Banks, near Cape Hatteras.

D This year, we'll Celebrate my birthday on the beach.

Go On ▶

12

F Our employees need a better place to eat his lunch.

G The cafeteria is having problems with its air conditioning.

H As a result, Carol and Wanda usually eat lunch at her desks.

J Sam and Eric sometimes go out to the parking lot to eat his lunches.

13

A I took my car to get its tires rotated at the service station.

B A mechanic told me that one tires tread was almost gone.

C Its only been a year since I replaced all four tires!

D I was lucky to buy a new set of tires' on sale.

14

F Mark our next-door neighbor, has a puppy.

G As soon as Mark gets home everyone knows it.

H The dog, a golden retriever, is already as big as a house.

J I hate to think of how big he will grow, they will need a bigger house.

15

A The meeting was held next October in Phoenix.

B Daniel set up the schedule as soon as he gets the dates.

C We fly to the meeting if the tickets are not too expensive.

D Cynthia will make the arrangements when she gets back from her vacation.

16

F My Sister and her husband were married ten years ago last Saturday.

G To celebrate their anniversary, they drove over the Mountains and to the Sea.

H It was the very first time that my Sister had seen the Pacific ocean.

J Her husband spent a lot of time watching the seals at Monterey Bay.

17

A A tax on e-mails, like a stamp on a letter?

B The e-mail tax is really just a hoax, however.

C After reading an interesting e-mail one morning.

D Sent from computer to computer all over the nation.

18

F As I was watching television last night; I saw that my team lost.

G Unfortunately, that means it is out of the playoffs now.

H By the way how are the Hawks doing in the playoffs?

J Despite their record this season they might win.

For numbers 19 through 24, read the paragraph. Then choose the sentence that best fills the blank in the paragraph.

19   Becoming a home health aide is not an easy career choice. The hours are long, and the pay is not exceptionally high. You often must deal with people who are in pain, depressed, or angry—definitely not at their best. _____.

    A Nevertheless, you are able to help them live healthier, happier lives.

    B For example, you are able to help them live healthier, happier lives.

    C In addition, you are able to help them live healthier, happier lives.

    D Therefore, you are able to help them live healthier, happier lives.

20   My uncle Ed started an exercise program about a month ago. First, he talked to his doctor about what kinds of exercise would be good for him, and his doctor gave him some pamphlets to read. _____. He has some sore muscles, but he says he feels better than he has in years.

    F Part of his program is walking two miles every day.

    G Now he has talked Aunt Dottie into exercising with him.

    H He wanted to become more fit and maybe lose some weight, too.

    J Then Uncle Ed set up a program that he has been following ever since.

21   _____. They spend years training to fly in the shuttles. They must know how to lead and how to be an effective team member, all at the same time. Astronauts must have nerves of steel in any emergency. Most of all, they must believe in their work so strongly that they are willing to risk their lives for it.

    A It's not easy to become an astronaut.

    B Many children hope to be astronauts.

    C Astronauts are truly special people.

    D Astronauts live exciting lives.

22   Jason decided that a resume would help him get a better job. After reading some tips about writing resumes, he went to the community library and used a computer there to write his own resume. _____. Finally, he went back to the library and printed his final draft on high-quality paper he had bought at an office-supply store.

    F Experts suggest using a high-quality paper for resumes.

    G During several job interviews, Jason was asked for his resume.

    H The computers are there for everyone, but often they are all being used.

    J Then he took it home and asked his parents to suggest changes.

23   _____. After a stress-filled day, it's a pleasure to run your hand over a nicely sanded piece of wood. Whether you use a small knife to carve animals or large power tools to frame a house, there is something satisfying about working with wood. The rewards of woodworking can range from a small keepsake to a comfortable home.

    A Ever since time began, people have made things from wood.

    B Even in our high-tech society, wood has many uses.

    C Woodworking is a relaxing, rewarding hobby.

    D Woodworking can be an inexpensive hobby.

24   Teaching children good eating habits is not easy these days. Children tend to pay more attention to how we adults eat than how we tell them to eat. _____. It's difficult, then, to convince them to eat only as much food as their bodies really need.

    F Similarly, they often see adults eat huge plates of food in restaurants.

    G However, they often see adults eat huge plates of food in restaurants.

    H For example, they often see adults eat huge plates of food in restaurants.

    J At the same time, they often see adults eat huge plates of food in restaurants.

For numbers 25 and 26, read the paragraph. Then choose the sentence that does <u>not</u> belong in the paragraph.

25   1. Some people believe that Abner Doubleday invented baseball in 1839. 2. However, baseball is actually based on a very old game called rounders. 3. At one time, there were two forms of baseball: the Massachusetts game, which allowed pitchers to throw overhand; and the New York game, which required pitchers to throw underhand. 4. Some people prefer playing baseball to watching it.

    A Sentence 1

    B Sentence 2

    C Sentence 3

    D Sentence 4

26   1. American soldiers played a form of baseball at Valley Forge in 1776. 2. That is the year that our nation won its independence from Great Britain. 3. Baseball became so popular that it was banned from the campus of Princeton University in 1787. 4. It was keeping the young students from their studies!

    F Sentence 1

    G Sentence 2

    H Sentence 3

    J Sentence 4

For numbers 27 through 33, read the letter and look at the numbered, underlined portions. Choose the answer that is written correctly for each underlined portion.

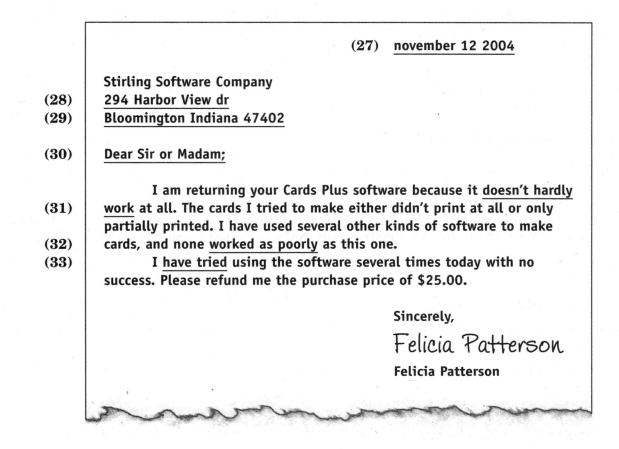

(27)   november 12 2004

Stirling Software Company
(28)   **294 Harbor View dr**
(29)   **Bloomington Indiana 47402**

(30)   **Dear Sir or Madam;**

      I am returning your Cards Plus software because it **doesn't hardly**
(31)   **work** at all. The cards I tried to make either didn't print at all or only
partially printed. I have used several other kinds of software to make
(32)   cards, and none **worked as poorly** as this one.
(33)   I **have tried** using the software several times today with no
success. Please refund me the purchase price of $25.00.

               Sincerely,

               Felicia Patterson

               Felicia Patterson

27 **A** November 12 2004
      B november 12, 2004
      C November 12, 2004
      D Correct as it is

28 **F** 294 Harbor View dr.
      G 294 Harbor View, Dr
      H 294 Harbor View Dr.
      J Correct as it is

29 **A** Bloomington Indiana, 47402
      B Bloomington, Indiana 47402
      C Bloomington, Indiana, 47402
      D Correct as it is

30 **F** Dear sir or madam:
      G Dear Sir or Madam:
      H Dear Sir or Madam,
      J Correct as it is

31 A hardly works
    B doesn't scarcely work
    C doesn't in no way work
    D Correct as it is

32 F worked as bad
    G worked worsely
    H was as worse working
    J Correct as it is

33 A has tried
    B have try
    C had tried
    D Correct as it is

For numbers 34 through 36, read the paragraph and look at the numbered, underlined portions. Choose the answer that is written correctly for each underlined portion.

(34) Do you procrastinate because you think you work better under stress? If so, experts say that you are fooling yourselve. You may get
(35) the work done but too much procrastination and stress can harm your
(36) health. You are also not likely to do your best work if procrastination is a problem for you, make a schedule and stick with it.

34 F yourself
    G yourselfs
    H yourselves
    J Correct as it is

35 A done, but
    B done but,
    C done; but
    D Correct as it is

36 F work, if
    G work. if
    H work. If
    J Correct as it is

For numbers 37 through 39, read the paragraph and look at the numbered, underlined portions. Choose the answer that is written correctly for each underlined portion.

> In the grocery store, is the largest size always the best buy?
> Many people think it is, but they need to consider how much they
> really need of a particular product. For example, are they going to
> (37)   eat that huge loaf of bread before <u>its stale</u>? Do they like green
> (38)   <u>beans enough</u> to eat a two-pound can of them? Sometimes, a
> (39)   <u>more small</u> can makes the most sense.

37
  A it stale
  B it's stale
  C its' stale
  D Correct as it is

39
  A smaller
  B most small
  C more smaller
  D Correct as it is

38
  F beans; enough
  G beans, enough
  H beans? Enough
  J Correct as it is

For numbers 40 through 42, choose the sentence that is written correctly <u>and</u> shows the correct capitalization and punctuation. Be sure the sentence you choose is complete.

40
  F Our building recently remodeled.
  G A small kitchen now with a microwave.
  H New carpeting and window blinds everywhere.
  J The employees appreciate the cleaner surroundings.

41
  A "Have you seen the new procedures for ordering supplies? Kyle asked."
  B Sarah asked "do you think they will cut down on mistakes?"
  C Hilda said, "I think there are a lot more forms now."
  D Pam told us "to start using the forms next week."

42
  F In July, Antonio is moving to Kansas city, Missouri.
  G Antonio already has an apartment on the north side of town.
  H He will work as a plumber's apprentice with his Brother, Oscar.
  J We are planning a huge Surprise Party for Antonio this saturday.

For numbers 43 through 45, read the paragraph and look at the numbered, underlined portions. Choose the answer that is written correctly for each underlined portion.

(43)   Would you like to work fewer hours and getting more done? Better
(44)   time management skills can help. This skills can help you identify
         how you spend your time and begin to control it. First you must set
(45)   priorities. Your "A" priorities should be urgently and important. Take
         care of these first to make the best use of your time.

43   **A** and when you get more done
         B and if you get more done
         C and get more done
         D Correct as it is

45   **A** urgently and importantly
         B urgent and importantly
         C urgent and important
         D Correct as it is

44   **F** That
         G These
         H Which
         J Correct as it is

For numbers 46 through 50, read the passage and look at the numbered, underlined portions. Choose the answer that is written correctly for each underlined portion.

(46)   Have you have ever worked in a sales position, if so, you have
         probably dealt with an angry customer. Many salespeople think
(47)   angry customers want their problems "fixed," but that is hardly never
         the case. Instead, customers want to be heard and listened to.
         "Fixing" the problem does not usually make angry customers
(48)   lesser angry. Instead, the salesperson should focus on the customers'
         feelings, saying something like, "It had to be frustrating when this
(49)   product didn't work." After the customer had settled down, the
         salesperson can deal with the problem. In dealing with customers
(50)   that are angry, calmness is always the key.

46   **F** position; if so
         G position. If so
         H position? If so,
         J Correct as it is

47   **A** not never
         B hardly ever
         C scarcely never
         D Correct as it is

48
F more lesser angry
G more less angry
H less angry
J Correct as it is

50
F who
G which
H what
J Correct as it is

49
A has settled
B was settled
C will have settled
D Correct as it is

For numbers 51 and 52, choose the answer that best develops the topic sentence.

51 Sometimes it's difficult to know when to go to the doctor.

A Doctor visits are increasingly expensive. Then lab tests and X-rays send the bill sky high.

B A family doctor can treat a wide range of illnesses in patients of all ages. However, at times you may need to see a specialist.

C Check to see if the doctor is qualified before you make an appointment. Ask your friends if they know, or have heard of, the doctor you have in mind.

D Symptoms that seem serious in the morning can disappear by the afternoon. Many illnesses go away on their own, so going to a doctor seems like a waste of time and money.

52 Some scientists believe that our weather patterns are changing.

F This past winter, Colorado experienced record-breaking snowfalls. Perhaps all that snow will help prevent a water shortage in that region this summer.

G Others think that every region on Earth naturally goes through periods of change. These scientists look at the long-term weather patterns and see no significant changes.

H Scientists who study climates are called climatologists. Scientists who study and predict the weather are called meteorologists.

J The weather has an immense effect on farming and crop production. Our unpredictable weather makes farming a risky business.

For numbers 53 through 55, choose the word or phrase that best completes the sentence.

53 My headache is _____ now than it was early this morning.

    A more badly

    B more bad

    C worse

    D worst

54 The shop _____ an hour earlier next Saturday.

    F open

    G will open

    H opens

    J opened

55 Employees _____ have been on the job for at least a year earn an extra day of vacation.

    A who

    B which

    C that

    D whom

STOP ✳

Lesson 1 Practice (page 9)

1. A The underlined words are the subject of the sentence. Therefore, the pronoun *I*, not *me*, is correct. Also, you should name yourself last. Option B (*Me and you*) and option D (*Correct as is*) are not correct because *Me* should not be used as a subject. Option C (*You and myself*) is not correct because *myself* should not be used as a subject.

2. F This word refers to a thing, the store, so *that* is correct. Option G (*whom*) and option H (*whose*) are not correct. These options relate to people, not things. The sentence is not correct as it is (option J).

3. C *Who* refers to a person, the owner, so it is the correct relative pronoun. Option A is an object pronoun. Options B and D refer to things or objects.

4. F The underlined word is the subject of the sentence. Therefore, the sentence requires *He* (we know from context earlier in the passage that the owner is a man). Option G is feminine. Option H is plural.

Lesson 2 Practice (page 11)

1. C This pronoun refers to *people*, so it must be plural. *Themselves* is plural. *Themself* (option A) is misspelled, and *himselves* (option B) is not a word. *Theirselves* (option D) is also not a word.

2. F This pronoun refers to *infection*, so it must be singular. *Itselves* (option G) and *theirselves* (option H) are not words. *Themselves* is not correct here because it is plural (option J).

3. A *Fact* is singular, so the singular pronoun *This* matches it. *Those* (option B) is incorrect because it is plural. *Which* (option C) does not make sense here. *These* is not correct here because it is plural (option D).

4. F In this sentence, it is not clear if the subject *you* is singular or plural, but *yourself* is the only correct pronoun choice. *Yourselfs* (option G), *yourselve* (option H), and *yourselve's* (option J) are all incorrect spellings.

Lesson 3 Practice (page 13)

1. B *Jill* is a singular noun that matches the singular pronoun *her*. In option A the plural noun *employees* does not match the singular pronoun *her*. In option C the gender-neutral noun *company* needs the gender-neutral pronoun *its*. In option D *Karl and John* is plural and *his* is singular.

2. H *Its* is correct because it is gender-neutral and singular, matching *company*. Option F is not correct because *his* is male and *Jill* is female. In option G *Karl and John* is plural and *her* is singular and female. Option J is not correct because *his* is singular.

3. B *Their* is a plural pronoun, so it matches the plural noun *companies*. In option A the pronoun should be female. In option C *his* does not match *employees*. In option D *Jill* and *Karl* are plural, and *his* is singular.

4. J *Karl* is singular and male, and so is *his*. In option F *people* is plural and *her* is singular. Option G needs *its* instead of *their*. In option H *Karl* requires a male pronoun.

5. A In option A *Karl* matches *his*. In option B *her* is singular when it should be plural. In option C *Karl and his family* does not match *its*. In option D *his* is singular when it should be plural.

6. G *Her* is a singular, female pronoun, so it matches the singular, female pronoun *she*. Option F is not correct because *his* is male. In option H *parents* does not match *his*. Option J is not correct because *her* is singular.

Lesson 4 Practice (page 15)

1. A Maria creates and begins in the present, so the present tense verb *begins* is correct. Option B is past tense, and option C is future tense. Option D is not correct because it is not the correct present tense form for the subject, Maria.

2. H *Will place* is future tense, describing what Maria will do with the plants after she finishes creating her plan. Option F is not correct because it is in the present tense, and option G is not correct because it is in the past tense. Option J is not correct because it is not future tense.

3. D Both verbs are in the present tense; the action is now. Options A, B, and C all contain incorrectly formed verbs. Option A should be *Her garden grows.* Option B should be *…her mom plants flowers.* Option C should be *Her family loves.*

4. J Both verbs are correct in the past tense. In option F, the verb should be future tense. In option G, the two verbs do not fit with each other. In option H, the words *All winter* indicate action in the past, and *now* indicates action in the present.

5. B When the subject is a person or an object, we add *s* to the end of a verb. Option A lacks the *s* ending. Option C is incorrect because it is future tense. Option D is incorrectly formed.

6. J When the subject is a person or an object, we add *s* to the end of a verb. Options F and H are the wrong tense for the sentence. Option G lacks the necessary *s* ending to fit with the subject.

1. C *Studies* is plural, so the helping verb should be plural: *have shown*. *Shown* (option A) needs a helping verb. "Recent studies *were shown*" (option B) does not make sense, because the studies were not shown anything. *Has shown* (option D) is not correct because the helping verb *has* is singular.

2. F *Are causing* is correct because the action is continuing. The sounds are already causing this problem, so options G and H are not correct. *Are caused* (option J) is not correct because it does not make sense in the sentence.

3. C The helping verb should be *have*. *Shouldn't been* (option A) does not have a helping verb. Option B incorrectly uses *of* as a helping verb. The verb is not correct as it is (option D) because it incorrectly uses *a* as a helping verb.

4. G The explorers *are using* the guns right now. *Had used* (option F) is incorrect because it indicates that the action is over. *Will be using* (option H) and *will have used* (option J) are both incorrect because they indicate that the action will take place in the future.

1. D The subject *One* is singular, so *is* is correct. Options A, B, and C are plural.

2. F The subject *information* is singular, so the verb should be singular. Options G, H, and J are plural.

3. A The subject *someone* is singular, so the verb should be singular. Options B, C, and D are plural.

4. F The subject *thieves* is plural, so the verb should be plural. Options G, H, and J are singular.

5. D The subject *they* is plural, so *change* is correct. Options A, B, and C are singular.

6. F The subject *you* takes a plural verb, so *notice* is correct. Options G, H, and J are singular.

1. D Option A should say "*setting* (putting dishes and utensils on) *the table*." Option B should say "*set* (put) *out the salad dressing*." Option C should say "*sit* (rest) *in each chair*."

2. G Option F should say "*everyone except* (but) *our toddler*." Option H should say "*No one except* (but) *the parents*." Option J should say that the children "*accept* (receive) *their tasks*."

3. C Option A should say "*sit* (rest) *around and play games*." Option B should say "*set* (put) *up an obstacle course*." Option D should say "*sitting* (resting) *in front of the TV*."

4. H Option F should say "*except for* (but) *Cynthia*." Option G should say "*accept* (receive) *new responsibilities*." Option J should say that the staff seems to "*accept* (receive) *John*."

5. A Option B should say "*He does not like to sit* (rest) *around*." Option C should say he has a hard time "*sitting* (resting) *through meetings*." Option D should say "*he likes to sit* (rest) *in the back of the room*."

6. F Option G should say when he "*accepted* (received) *the job*." Option H should say he "*accepted* (received) *two weeks of vacation*." Option J should say "*except for* (but) *on sunny days*."

1. B This sentence compares one bone to all the other bones found, so *biggest* is correct. *Bigger* (option A) is not correct because it is in the form that compares only two things. *More big* (option C) and *most big* (option D) are not correct superlative forms.

2. F This sentence compares two things: reality and our expectations. *Smaller* is correct. *More small* (option G) and *most small* (option H) are not correct comparative forms. *Smallest* (option J) compares more than two things.

3. C *More massive* is correct because this sentence compares two things: the weight of a sauropod and the total weight of five elephants. *Massiver* (option A) and *massivest* (option B) are not correct adjectives. *Most massive* (option D) is incorrect because it is in the form that compares more than two things.

4. J *Deeper* is correct because this sentence compares two positions. *Deepest* (option F) is not correct because it is in the form that compares more than two things. *More deep* (option G) and *most deep* (option H) are not correct adjectives.

1. B *Safely* requires the word *less*. Option A makes the sentence unclear. *Less safelier* (option C) and *safelier* (option D) are not correct comparative forms.

2. H The adverb *often* requires the word *less*. Option F makes the sentence unclear. *Oftener* (option G) and *less oftener* (option J) are not correct comparative forms.

3. A *More* and *-er* should not be used with *less*, making options B, C, and D incorrect.

4. G The plural subject *people* needs the plural verb *are*. Option F is plural but past tense. Options H and J are singular.

5. B The sentence calls for present tense. Option A is not correct because it indicates that the act of including is ongoing. Option C is past perfect tense, and option D is future tense.

6. F *Less* should not be combined with *more, most,* or *-er*, making options G, H, and J incorrect.

1. A The adjective *serious* is correct because it describes the degree of seriousness of the *ticket*. Option B is not a word. Option C does not make sense in the sentence. Option D is an adverb.

2. F The adverb *usually* is correct because it describes the verb *involve*. Option G is not a word. Option H makes a comparison, but nothing is being compared in this sentence. Option J is an adjective.

3. C The adverbs *quickly and easily* are correct because they describe the verb *can send*. The words in option A are adjectives. Options B and D each have one adverb and one adjective.

4. F This sentence uses the adjective *worse* to compare drunk driving with other traffic violations. *Worse* is the form of *bad* that is used in comparisons. Option G is not a word. Option H is a comparative adverb form. Option J is not a correct use of *bad*.

5. A These adjectives describe the noun *ticket*. Options B and D each contain one adjective and one adverb. Both words in option C are adverbs.

6. G *Badly* is an adverb that describes the adjective *injured*. Option F incorrectly uses the adjective *bad* to describe the adjective *injured*. Option H seems to be comparing injuries, which does not make sense here. *Worsely* in option J is not a word.

Lesson 11 Practice (page 29)

1. A This option has only one negative: *hardly*. Option B has *won't* and *hardly*, option C has *not* and *never*, and option D has *not* and *hardly*.

2. J This option has only one negative: *won't*. Option F has *won't* and *never*, option G has *not* and *never*, and option H has *not* and *hardly*.

3. A This option has only one negative: *not*. Option B has *not* and *barely*, option C has *can't* and *hardly*, and option D has *don't* and *never*.

4. H This option has only one negative: *Don't*. Option F has *not* and *never*, option G has *Don't* and *none*, and option J has *not* and *scarcely*.

5. A This option has only one negative: *isn't*. Option B has *not* and *neither*, option C has *isn't* and *never*, and option D has *isn't* and *no*.

6. H This option has only one negative: *Never*. Option F has *don't* and *no*, option G has *don't* and *no one*, and option J has *not* and *never*.

TABE Review: Usage (pages 30–31)

1. A The subject *jobs* is plural, so the verb should be plural: *are*. The verbs in options B, C, and D are singular. [Subject and Verb Agreement]

2. F This word describes the verb *is handled*, so it should be the adverb *usually*. Options G, H, and J are adjectives or are incorrectly formed. [Choosing Between Adjectives and Adverbs]

3. B Option A is plural, which is not correct here. Option C is also plural and misspelled. Option D is misspelled. [Reflexive and Demonstrative Pronouns]

4. G This option has only one negative, *not*. Option F has *don't* and *never*, option H has *Don't* and *no*, and option J has *not* and *never*. [Using Negatives]

5. D *Kinds* is plural and so is *these*. *This* (option A) and *That* (option B) are incorrect because they are singular. *Which* (option C) does not make sense here. [Reflexive and Demonstrative Pronouns]

6. F *Has started* is correct for an action that began in the past and continues. Option G suggests that the action began in the past and stopped. Options H and J do not make sense. [Perfect and Progressive Tenses]

7. C The relative pronoun *who* refers to people. The words in options A, B, and D all refer to things or objects. [Nominative and Relative Pronouns]

8. G The sentence requires a present tense verb. The correct form for a plural subject, *candidates*, is *mail*. Option F is future tense. Option H is past tense. Option J is not the correct form for a plural subject. [Present and Future Tenses]

9. A Both verbs in option A are in future tense. Option B is incorrectly in the past tense. Option C has two verbs whose tenses don't fit with each other. Option D has an incorrectly formed future tense verb. [Present and Future Tenses]

10. G *Sit* is used correctly to mean "rest in a chair." Option F should say "*except* the job salary." Option H should say "*Set* your handbag." Option J should say "to *accept* the job." [Easily Confused Verbs]

11. D The singular pronoun *its* agrees with the singular noun *company*. Option A should say "*their* resumes." Option B should say "*their* interviews." Option C should say "*their* files." [Antecedent Agreement]

12. F In options G and J, *has* should be *have*. In option H, the verb should have an *-ing* ending. [Perfect and Progressive Tenses]

13. A The adjective *important* requires the adverb *less*. *More less* (option B) and *most less* (option C) are not correct comparative adverb forms. Option D is not correct because it does not make a comparison. [Comparative Adverbs]

14. H *Whom* is the object of the preposition *to*. *Who* (option F) should not be used as an object. *What* (option G) and *which* (option J) should not be used to refer to a person. [Nominative and Relative Pronouns]

15. B *You* and *I* are the correct pronouns to use as a subject. Option A is incorrect because you should name yourself last. *Me* (options C and D) should not be used as a subject. [Nominative and Relative Pronouns]

16. H This sentence compares more than two things; it compares one interview to all other interviews, so *most difficult* is correct. It is not correct to add *-er* (option F) or *-est* (option G) to a long adjective. Option J should be used to compare only two things. [Comparative and Superlative Adjectives]

1. B Option A is a run-on that should be separated between *car* and *a*. Options C and D are fragments.

2. H Options F and G are fragments. Option J is a run-on that should be separated between *pools* and *find*.

3. B Options A and C are fragments. Option D is a run-on that should be separated between *clean* and *protect*.

4. H Options F and G are fragments. Option J is a run-on that should be separated between *stations* and *don't*.

5. C The first group of words in the paragraph is a run-on that should be separated with a period after *automobile*. Options A, B, and D are not correct because they are also run-ons.

6. J Options F, G, and H are not correct, as no punctuation is needed within this complete, correct sentence.

1. A Option B is not correct because the word *heavy* is misplaced. Options C and D are not the best choices because the sentences use extra unnecessary words.

2. G Option F is not correct because "*from cars, trucks, and buses*" is incorrectly placed in the sentence. Option H is not correct because it does not make sense. Option J is not correct because it does not mention the pollution.

3. B Option A is not the best sentence combination because it uses extra unnecessary words. Option C and Option D are both not correct because "*television*" is incorrectly placed in each one.

4. F Option F is the only option that places *serious* in the correct position in the sentence. In option G, the adjective *serious* modifies *air pollution* instead of *asthma*, as intended. Option H places *seriously* in the wrong position in the sentence. Option J is not the best choice because it uses extra unnecessary words.

5. B Option A is not correct because the word *dark* is misplaced. Option C is not correct because *tiny* and *dark* are misplaced. Option D uses extra, unnecessary words.

1. A This sentence joins the subjects and states the verb once. Option B includes both the subject and *they*, a pronoun that should take the place of a subject. Option C repeats the verb *cost*. Option D unnecessarily repeats many words.

2. G This sentence joins the subjects and states the verb once. Option F omits the names of the libraries. Option H is a run-on sentence. Option J unnecessarily repeats many words.

3. B This sentence joins the subjects and states the verb once. Option A is an awkward and wordy way to combine these sentences. Option C changes

the meaning of the two sentences. Option D unnecessarily repeats many words.

4. F This sentence joins the subjects and states the verb once. Option G includes both the subject and *they*, a pronoun that should take the place of a subject. Option H is an awkward and wordy way to combine these sentences. Option J unnecessarily repeats many words.

5. A This sentence joins the subjects and states the verb once. Option B repeats the verb *takes*. Option C changes the meaning of the two sentences. Option D unnecessarily repeats many words.

1. B This option combines both sentences without changing their meaning. Option A suggests that Christopher was an electrician while he was at a trade school. Option C combines the sentences in a confusing way. Option D repeats or adds too many words.

2. G This option combines both sentences without changing their meaning. Options F, H, and J all change the meaning of the original sentences.

3. A This option combines two equally important ideas with the word *and*. Options B, C, and D confuse the two ideas and change the meaning of the original sentences.

4. H This option combines the two sentences without changing their meaning. Options F, G, and J suggest that Kevin either wants to graduate, will graduate, or is now graduating. The original sentence says he just graduated.

1. B In option B it is clear that Jenny, not her dad, is the one who was 12 at the time her dad remarried. Option A is a run-on sentence. Option C is not correct because it suggests that Jenny's dad was 12 when he remarried. In option D, it is unclear who was 12, Jenny or her dad.

2. F Option F makes it clear that the snowflakes are falling gently outside the window. In option G, the words *falling gently outside the window* immediately follow *We*, which gives the sentence the meaning that the speaker and his wife were falling outside the window. In option H, the words *of the year* are incorrectly separated from the word they describe, *snowflakes*. In option J, it is not clear what is falling outside the window.

3. D It is clear that *with a beautiful voice* should follow and describe *A soloist*. Option A contains a sentence fragment, *A few songs*, and is therefore incorrect. Option B is not correct because *with a beautiful voice* follows *songs*. The songs don't have the beautiful voice; the singer does. Option C includes a sentence fragment, *Sang a few songs*.

4. H In option H, it is clear that the speaker and his wife saw the wedding cake as they were walking past the

table. Including *We* and *it* as subjects helps make the sentence clear. In option F, the wedding cake is looking delicious and walking past the table. In option G, the cake is walking. In option J, it is not clear what is walking.

5. A Placing *with a great saxophone player* right after *band* leaves no doubt that it's the band that has the great player. In option B, the words *with a great saxophone player* follow *music*. This word order means that the music has a great saxophone player, not the band. Option C includes a sentence fragment. In option D, *with a great saxophone player* follows *dancing*. This word order suggests that people at the wedding were *dancing with* the saxophone player.

6. G In this choice, the word *almost* is placed next to *midnight*. This means that the speaker and his wife stayed at the reception until about 11:45 p.m. In option F, it is unclear what the word *almost* refers to. In option H, it is not clear what the sentence means because the placement of *almost* is confusing. In option J, *almost* is next to *stayed* rather than *midnight*. Therefore, the meaning is that the speaker almost stayed at the reception, but then didn't.

Lesson 17 Practice (page 43)

1. A *Has heard* has the same grammatical structure as the past tense verb, *has received*. Options B, C, and D are not past tense verbs.

2. H *To add* has the same grammatical structure as *to send* and *to remove*. Options F, G, and J are all different structures.

3. C *By phoning* has the same grammatical structure as *by mailing*. Options A, B, and D are not the same structure as *by mailing*.

4. F *Break* has the same grammatical structure as the present tense verb, *are*. Options G, H, and J are not present tense verbs.

5. B *They do not get rich* has the same grammatical structure as *People…receive little or nothing in return*. Options A, C, and D are all different structures.

6. H *Contact them* has the same grammatical structure as *call the U.S. Postal Inspection Service*. Options F, G, and J are all different structures.

TABE Review: Sentence Formation (page 44)

1. C This should all be one sentence, so there should be a comma after *skin,* and *Don't* should not be capitalized. In option A, there should be a comma after *skin*. In option B, the comma is in the wrong place. As written, the sentence includes a fragment (option D). [Sentence Recognition]

2. F Parallel structure would be *remove the tick and kill any germs*. Options G, H, and J do not have parallel structure. [Nonparallel Structure]

3. C This option makes it clear that the person removing the tick is doing the grasping. The word order in options A, B, and D all seem to indicate that the tick is doing the grasping.

4. G *Slowly* tells how to pull on the tick. In options F and H, the sentence says the tick will slowly let go. Option J combines the sentences in a confusing way. [Adding Modifiers to Combine Sentences]

5. A In option A, the subjects are combined and the verb is stated once. Options B, C, and D combine the sentences awkwardly and/or repeat words. [Compounding]

Lesson 18 Practice (page 46)

1. C Option C introduces the topic of the paragraph. Option A is about medical bills, not coverage. Option B is about complications, not coverage. Option D is true, but it's not the topic of the paragraph.

2. J The paragraph is about the doctor's personality. Options F, G, and H are not about personality.

3. B The paragraph is about choosing a doctor for a child. Option A is too broad a topic, while options C and D are too narrow in focus.

4. G The paragraph consists of questions about the doctor's practice. Options F, J, and H could be included in the paragraph, but they are too narrow in focus to be the topic sentence.

Lesson 19 Practice (page 48)

1. A These sentences add more information about Matera. Options B, C, and D do not offer information about the 2002 tour or Matera.

2. J These sentences offer more information about the controls, but options F, G, and H do not.

3. C These sentences provide more information about the course, but options A, B, and D do not.

4. H These sentences tell how to find more information about the Park World Tour, but options F, G, and J do not.

Lesson 20 Practice (page 50)

1. B Option B fits here and leads smoothly to the next sentence. Option A is not on the correct topic, while option C fits better at the end of the paragraph. Option D fits with option A, but not in this paragraph.

2. G This sentence carries on the topic of the previous sentence by describing a second way that tires can lose air pressure. Option F is slightly off the topic, and option H might be used in a following paragraph. Option J fits better as the third sentence in the paragraph.

3. C This sentence adds more information about underinflated tires, which were mentioned in the previous sentence. Option A is not needed in the paragraph. Option B would be better as the third sentence in the paragraph, and option D should be the last sentence in the paragraph.

4. J This sentence tells more about how to place the penny. Option F might be used as the first sentence in the paragraph. Option G might come after the current first sentence in the paragraph. Option H tells more about indicators and should follow the current third sentence.

1. A This sentence contradicts the idea that some Web sites are trustworthy. Option B suggests that this sentence is similar to an earlier one. Option C suggests that this sentence is the result of an earlier one. Option D suggests that this sentence is in defiance of an earlier one.

2. J An increase in scams is the result of the growth of the Internet. Option F says scam artists use the Internet in addition to something else. Option G says they use the Internet despite its popularity. Option H suggests that scam artists have taken a long time to begin using the Internet.

3. B *Therefore* suggests that you are safe because these ads are probably legitimate. Option A suggests that you are safe despite these ads being legitimate. Option C suggests that the sentence is similar to an earlier one. Option D says you are safe at last.

Lesson 22 Practice (page 54)

1. C The paragraph is not about the Food Guide Pyramid. Options A, B, and D all belong in the paragraph because they are all about bread in lunches.

2. G The paragraph is not about the vitamins in vegetables. Options F, H, and J all belong in the paragraph because they are about getting children to eat vegetables.

3. D The paragraph is not about tryouts. Options A, B, and C all belong in the paragraph because they are about packing notes in lunches.

4. H The paragraph is not about neatness. Options F, G, and J all belong in the paragraph because they are about avoiding food poisoning.

TABE Review: Paragraph Development (page 55)

1. D This sentence states the specific topic of the paragraph. Options A, B, and C are too general to be the topic sentence. [Topic Sentence]

2. G Patients are home sooner *as a result* of the shorter healing time. Plus, this sentence about going home makes sense after the sentence about a shorter healing period. Option F incorrectly suggests a contradiction. Option J incorrectly suggests a contradiction and is out of sequence. Option H incorrectly suggests an addition or comparison and is out of sequence. [Connective and Transition Words]

3. B The sentences in option B offer more details about how the surgery is performed. The sentences in options A, C, and D do not discuss this new technique. [Supporting Sentences]

4. J The paragraph is not about patients' preferences. Options F, G, and H all belong in the paragraph because they are about the doctor and his new technique. [Unrelated Sentences]

Lesson 23 Practice (page 57)

1. A In option C, *helping* should be capitalized because it is the first word of a sentence. Option B creates a run-on sentence. Option D is not correct because *helping* should be capitalized.

2. J *Owen National Forest* is the name of a specific place, so all of the words should be capitalized. Options F, G, and H lack capital letters on some or all of the words.

3. A The first word and the name of a specific place are correctly capitalized. In option B, *Citizens* should not be capitalized. In option C, *saturday* should be capitalized. In option D, *february* needs to be capitalized.

4. J The first word and the important words in the name of a literary work are capitalized. In option F, *River* does not need a capital letter because it does not refer to a specific river. Option G lacks a capital letter for the first word. In option H, *City* should not be capitalized.

5. D The first word and the name of a month are correctly capitalized. Options A, B, and C all contain words that are incorrectly capitalized: *School, Western,* and *River,* respectively.

Lesson 24 Practice (page 59)

1. C This question requires a question mark. The endmarks in options A, B, and D are not used to punctuate a question.

2. H This statement should end with a period. Options F and G create run-on sentences, while option J is incorrect because it ends a statement with a question mark.

3. B This sentence expresses a strong feeling and should end with an exclamation point. The endmarks in options A, C, and D are not used to express strong emotion.

4. H This question should end with a question mark. Options F, G, and J are not used to punctuate a question.

5. A This statement should end with a period. Options B, C, and D are not used to punctuate a statement.

6. G This sentence expresses a strong feeling and should end with an exclamation point. Options F, H, and J are not used to punctuate an exclamation.

Lesson 25 Practice (page 61)

1. C *Keith's new manager* should be set off on both sides with a comma. Putting a period (option A) or a semicolon (option B) after *Hershey* creates a fragment. As it is written (option D), the sentence needs a comma after *manager.*

2. F A comma after *After that* correctly separates the introductory element from the rest of the sentence. Options G and H contain incorrectly placed commas.

3. C In option C, the semicolon separates the parts of the compound sentence and a comma separates

however from the rest of the sentence. In option A, the comma is missing. In option B, there should be a semicolon in place of the first comma. With no punctuation (option D), the sentence is a run-on.

4. J The sentence is correct as it is written, with a comma following the introductory phrase *Before long*. In option F, the comma is in the wrong place. In option G, the comma is missing. In option H, there is a semicolon where there should be a comma.

5. B In option B, the words at the beginning of the sentence are correctly set off with a comma. In option A, there should be a comma after *Still*. In option C, there should be a comma after *carefully*, and in option D, there should be a comma after *time*.

6. H This sentence should have a comma after *Keith*. It does not need a semicolon (option F) or a period (option G), and it is incorrect without the comma (option J).

TABE Review: Capitalization and Punctuation (page 62)

1. B The first sentence is a statement and should end with a period. The first word of the next sentence should be capitalized. Options A and D create run-on sentences. Option C ends a statement with a question mark. [End Marks]

2. J *The person who interviewed you* renames Ms. Baker and is correctly set off with a comma. In option F, the comma is missing. Options G and H create sentence fragments. [Commas and Semicolons]

3. C A semicolon can be used to end the first sentence, and the phrase *in fact* should be set off with a comma. Option A is missing the comma. Options B and D create run-on sentences. [Commas and Semicolons]

4. G This option is correct because it begins with a capital letter and it does not include any unnecessary capitalization. In option F, the first word should be capitalized and *Thank-You* should not be capitalized. In option H, *Thank-You Note* should not be capitalized. The sentence is not correct as it is (option J) because it begins with a lowercase letter. [Capitalization]

5. A The introductory words *Above all* are correctly followed by a comma. In option B, *Company* should not be capitalized. In option C, a comma should follow *Corey*, and *Month* should not be capitalized. In option D, *No* should be followed by a comma, and *february* should be capitalized and followed by a comma. [Commas and Semicolons]

6. H Option H begins with a capital letter and is punctuated correctly. Option F is not correct because *Boss* should not be capitalized. Option G is not correct because *Time Clock* should not be capitalized. In option J, there should not be a comma after *right*. [Capitalization]

Lesson 26 Practice (page 64)

1. B This quotation needs an ending quotation mark. Option A is also missing the ending quotation mark and should have a comma instead of the period. Option C uses a question mark to end a statement. Option D is missing the ending quotation mark.

2. G *Sleeping* begins a new sentence and should begin with a capital letter. Option F is missing the beginning quotation mark, and option H should have a period in place of the comma. In option J, *sleeping* should be capitalized.

3. A This quotation is a statement and should end with a period. The punctuation marks in options B and C are not needed, but the sentence does need a period, making it incorrect as written (option D).

4. G A comma should follow *said* and separate these words from the quotation. Neither a period (option F) nor a question mark (option H) is needed. The missing comma makes the sentence incorrect as written (option J).

5. C Option C is punctuated correctly. In options A and D, an ending quotation mark is needed. In option B, *those* should begin with a capital letter.

6. H Option H is punctuated correctly. In option F, there should be a comma after *said*. In option G, there should be a question mark after *application*, not a period. In option J, *it* should be capitalized.

Lesson 27 Practice (page 66)

1. D Option D is correct because it is (*it's*) easy to find these people. Option A is not correct because *its* is the possessive form. In option B, the apostrophe is in the wrong place. In option C, the tense is changed, making the sentence confusing.

2. H The writer is describing one friend, and adding *'s* makes *friend* possessive. Option F does not show possession. In option G, *friends'* means ownership by more than one friend. Option J is incorrect because *friends* requires an apostrophe.

3. A In option A, *its* shows possession. Option B is not correct because *its'* has an apostrophe. Option C does not make sense. Option D is not correct because *it's* is the contraction of "it is."

4. H In option H, *It's* needs the apostrophe because it is a contraction. In option F, *goals'* should not end with an apostrophe. In option G, *neighbor's* would correctly show possession. In option J, *it's* should be *its* to show possession.

5. C In option C, *it's* is correct with the apostrophe because it is a contraction of "it is." In option A, *people's* would be correct. In option B, *Its* should be *It's*. In option D, the singular possessive *friend's* would be correct.

6. F In option F, *it's* is a contraction. In option G, *its* should be *it's*. In option H, *Experts* should be possessive: *Experts'*. In option J, *priorities* should not have an apostrophe because it is not possessive.

1. **D** Option A is missing the comma after the day. In option B, the comma is in the wrong place. In option C, *may* should be capitalized.

2. **H** In option F, *st* should be capitalized and end with a period. In option G, the period is missing. In option J, *st.* should be capitalized.

3. **A** Option B should have a comma after *Denver* instead of *Colorado*. Option C has an extra comma after *Colorado*. In option D, there should be a comma after *Denver*.

4. **H** Option F is too personal for a business letter. Option G should end with a colon. Option J should not end with a comma.

5. **C** In option A, *sincerely* should be capitalized, and a comma should be used instead of a colon. In option B, *Yours* should not be capitalized, and a comma should follow the closing. In option D, *Yours* should not be capitalized.

TABE Review: Writing Conventions (page 69)

1. **C** In option A, the comma after the day is missing. In option B, *august* should be capitalized. In option D, the comma should be after the day, not the month. [Parts of a Letter]

2. **H** In option F, *ave* should be capitalized and followed by a period. In option G, *ave.* should be capitalized. In option J, *Ave* should be followed by a period. [Parts of a Letter]

3. **C** A comma correctly separates *she said* from the quotation. In option A, the comma and beginning quotation mark are missing. In option B, there should be a comma instead of a period. In option D, the comma after *said* is missing. [Quotation Marks]

4. **J** A period correctly ends the quotation, followed by the ending quotation mark. In option F, the ending quotation mark is missing. In option G, the period is missing. Option H should use a period instead of a comma. [Quotation Marks]

5. **B** *Neighbor's* is a singular possessive noun, to match the singular *Patty Thomas*. In option A, *neighbors'* is the plural possessive form. Option C has too many *s's*. In option D, the apostrophe is missing. [Apostrophes]

6. **J** The possessive form is correct. In option F, *its'* is not a word. Options G and H do not make sense in the sentence. [Apostrophes]

TABE Review: Spelling (pages 73–74)

1. **B** The correct spelling is *attendance*. *Attendants* (option D) is spelled correctly, but it means "helpers" and that meaning does not make sense in this sentence. Options A and C are misspelled. [Structural Units]

2. **G** The correct spelling is *treasurer*. Options F, H, and J are misspelled. [Vowels]

3. **B** The correct spelling is *petition*. The schwa sound is in the first syllable. Options A, C, and D are misspelled. [Vowels]

4. **J** The correct spelling is *courteous*. Options F, G, and H are misspelled. [Vowels]

5. **C** The correct spelling is *twelfth*. Options A, B, and D are misspelled. [Structural Units]

6. **H** The correct spelling is *signature*. The schwa sound is in the second syllable. Options F, G, and J are misspelled. [Vowels]

7. **A** The second syllable of *rebel* is stressed (said louder), so you double the last consonant before adding the ending *-ion*: rebel+l+ion. Options B, C, and D are misspelled. [Consonants]

8. **J** The correct spelling is *mortgage*. Options F, G, and H are misspelled. [Consonants]

9. **B** The correct spelling is *existence*. Options A, C, and D are misspelled. [Structural Units]

10. **J** *Cereal* is eaten for breakfast. A *serial* (option F) is something that appears in parts, like a television series. Options G and H are misspelled. [Structural Units]

11. **C** The correct spelling is *leisure*. In options A, B, and D, the long vowel is misspelled. [Vowels]

12. **H** The suffix *-ous* is spelled correctly in option H. In options F, G, and J, the suffix is misspelled. [Structural Units]

13. **B** The correct spelling for the meaning of the sentence is *vane*. Options A and C are not a correct spelling in the context of this sentence. Option A is a correct spelling of *vein*, meaning blood vessel, and Option C is a correct spelling of *vain*, meaning having excessively high regard for oneself. Option D is misspelled. [Structural Units]

14. **H** The correct spelling is *competent*. Similar word parts in words like *insistent*, *consistent*, and *content* offer clues to the spelling of *competent*. Options F, G, and J are misspelled. [Structural Units]

15. **C** In option C, the variant spelling for the *sh* sound is spelled correctly with *-ti*. Options A, B, and D are misspelled. [Consonants]

16. **F** The correct spelling is *eligible*. Similar word parts in words like *negligible* and *incorrigible* offer clues to the spelling of *eligible*. Options G, H, and J are misspelled. [Structural Units]

17. **A** The schwa sound in the second syllable is spelled correctly in option A. The schwa sound is misspelled in options B, C, and D. [Vowels]

18. **G** The root of the word is spelled correctly in option G. Options F, H, and J are misspelled. [Structural Units]

19. **C** The r-controlled vowel is spelled correctly in option C. Options A, B, and D are misspelled. [Vowels]

20. **J** The silent letter is spelled correctly in option J. Options F, G, and H are misspelled. [Consonants]

A. C This sentence is complete and has no errors. In option A, *Manufacturing Plant* should not be capitalized. Option B is a fragment; it is missing a verb. In option D, *Every morning* and *regularly* are repetitious.

B. G *Blue* describes *shirts*, so it should be placed before *shirts*. Option F places *blue* incorrectly, while options H and J repeat words.

C. C The correct answer has a question mark at the end of the first sentence and a capital letter beginning the second sentence. In option A, a question mark should replace the period. Option B is a run-on sentence because it does not include the correct punctuation to end the first sentence. Option D is not correct because the second sentence needs to begin with a capital *I*.

D. F Option F has correct punctuation and capitalization. Option G should end with a question mark, not a period. Option H is not correct because it does not have an ending punctuation mark. In option J, *wednesday* should be capitalized.

1. B *Evan* should be followed by a comma because the speaker is talking to him. The punctuation marks in options A and C are not needed in this sentence, but a comma is necessary, making option D incorrect. [Commas and Semicolons]

2. F This sentence is a statement and should end with a period. Options G and H are not needed, but the period is necessary, making option J incorrect. [End Marks]

3. C An ending quotation mark should follow the question mark. Options A and B are not needed. But the quotation marks are, so option D is incorrect. [Quotation Marks]

4. H *From Chicago* describes the supervisor. Option F makes it seem that the assembly lines are from Chicago, while option G suggests the plant is from Chicago. Option J repeats too many words. [Adding Modifiers to Combine Sentences]

5. B The original sentences say that the buildings were old and battered. Option A repeats too many words. In options C and D, *old* and *battered* incorrectly describe the wind and the town. [Adding Modifiers to Combine Sentences]

6. F This sentence combines the subjects and states the verb once, but options G, H, and J repeat too many words. [Compounding]

7. B This sentence connects these two ideas in a way that makes sense. Option A makes it seem that one thing *or* the other will happen. Option C is incorrect because the building was opened first, and the plant may hire new workers. Option D confuses the two ideas. [Coordinating and Subordinating]

8. F This sentence has no errors. In option G, *march* should be capitalized, and in option H, *Birthday* should not be capitalized. In option J, *Company* and *Month* should not be capitalized. [Capitalization]

9. D This sentence contains no errors. The other three all contain misplaced modifiers. Option A implies that the television was walking through the door. Option B indicates that the person locked their hat to the bike rack. Option C says that the commuter van beeped its horn after eating breakfast. [Misplaced Modifiers]

10. H This sentence contains no errors. In options F and J, *accept* should be *except*. In option G, *excepted* should be *accepted*. [Easily Confused Verbs]

11. B This sentence contains no errors. *Summer* in option A and *Southern* in option C should not be capitalized. In option D, *Celebrate* should not be capitalized. [Capitalization]

12. G The singular *its* matches the singular *cafeteria*. In option F, *his* should be *their* to match *employees*. In option H, *her* should be *their* to match *Carol and Wanda*. In option J, *his* should be *their* to match *Sam and Eric*. [Antecedent Agreement]

13. A The possessive form, *its*, is correct here. In option B, *tires* should be *tire's*. In option C, *Its* should be *It's*, the contraction. In option D, *tires'* should not have an apostrophe because this word is not possessive; nothing belongs to the tires. [Apostrophe]

14. H *A golden retriever* is correctly set off by commas because it renames *The dog*. Option F should have a comma after *Mark,* and option G should have one after *home*. Option J should have a semicolon, not a comma, after *grow* to separate the two sentences. [Commas and Semicolons]

15. D This sentence uses the future tense correctly. Option A should say *will be held*. Option B should say *will set up*, and option C should say *will fly*. [Present and Future Tenses]

16. J This sentence has no errors. In option F, *Sister* should not be capitalized. In option G, *Mountains* and *Sea* should not be capitalized because they are not names of specific places. In option H, *Sister* should not be capitalized again, but *ocean* should be because it's part of the name of a specific place or geological term. [Capitalization]

17. B This is a complete sentence, but options A, C, and D are fragments. [Sentence Recognition]

18. G This sentence correctly has a comma after the introductory word. Option F should have a comma (not a semicolon) after *night*, as this is one sentence. Option H should have a comma after *way*, and option J needs one after *season*. [Commas and Semicolons]

19. A *Nevertheless* correctly shows that this sentence contradicts the previous ones. This sentence is not an example (option B) or similar to another point (option C). Neither is it the result of a previous point (option D). [Connective and Transition Words]

20. J This sentence fits into this sequence of events. Option F would fit in a paragraph that describes the details of Ed's exercise program. Option G might fit at the end of this paragraph. Option H would be better as the second sentence in the paragraph. [Sequence]

21. C This sentence introduces the topic of the paragraph: the unique qualities that astronauts must have. Option A suggests that the paragraph is about how someone becomes an astronaut. Option B implies that the paragraph is about children, while option D suggests that it is about the excitement of being an astronaut. [Topic Sentence]

22. J This sentence continues the sequence of events. Options F and H are slightly off the topic. Option G would be better at the beginning of the paragraph. [Sequence]

23. C This sentence introduces the true topic, while option A implies that the paragraph is about the history of using wood. Option B suggests that it's about the current uses of wood, and option D implies that it's about the cost of the hobby. [Topic Sentence]

24. H This sentence offers an *example* of how adults eat. The connective words that begin options F, G, and J do not make sense here. [Connective and Transition Words]

25. D The last sentence is off the topic of baseball history. Options A, B, and C all provide information about the history of baseball. [Unrelated Sentences]

26. G This sentence is about our nation's history, not baseball history. Options F, H, and J all provide information about the history of baseball. [Unrelated Sentences]

27. C This is the correct format for a date. Option A needs a comma after *12*, and *november* should be capitalized in option B. The date is not correct as is (option D). [Parts of a Letter]

28. H This is the correct format for a street address. In option F, *dr.* should be capitalized. Option G needs no comma after *View*, but it does need a period after *Dr*. The address is not correct as is (option J). [Parts of a Letter]

29. B This is the correct format for a city and state. In option A, the comma should follow *Bloomington*, not *Indiana,* and option C has an extra comma after *Indiana*. This part of the address is not correct without the comma (option D). [Parts of a Letter]

30. G This is the correct format for a business letter greeting. In option F, *sir* and *madam* should be capitalized. The greeting should end with a colon, not a comma (option H) or a semicolon (option J). [Parts of a Letter]

31. A This option contains only one negative: *hardly*. Options B, C, and D all contain two negatives. [Using Negatives]

32. J *Poorly* is an adverb, describing how the software worked. Option F uses the adjective *bad*. In option G, *worsely* is not a word, while option H is also incorrect. [Choosing Between Adjectives and Adverbs]

33. D In this sentence, the present perfect tense is used to express action that started in the past and continues into the present. In options A and C, the helping verb is not correct. In option B, *try* should be *tried*. [Perfect and Progressive Tenses]

34. F This is the correct spelling, but options G and J are spelled incorrectly. Option H uses the plural form, which is incorrect here. [Reflexive and Demonstrative Pronouns]

35. A This compound sentence needs a comma between the main parts. Option B puts the comma in the wrong place. The semicolon in option C should not be used with a conjunction (*but*). Option D, with no comma, is a run-on. [Compounding]

36. H *Work* ends a sentence and should be followed by a period. *If* begins another sentence and should be capitalized. Options F and J create run-ons. In option G, *if* should be capitalized. [Capitalization]

37. B The contraction *it's* is correct here. Option A is missing the helping verb *is*. Option C has the apostrophe in the wrong place, while option D uses the possessive form, *its*. [Apostrophes]

38. J This is one sentence, so no punctuation is needed here. Options F and H divide the sentence, creating a fragment, and option G has an unnecessary comma. [Sentence Recognition]

39. A This sentence compares two sizes of cans. Option B is incorrect because two things are being compared; *-est* would be added to *small* if more than two were being compared. Using *more* plus the *-er* ending (option C) is incorrect. *Small* is a short word, so we add *-er*, not *more* (option D). [Comparative and Superlative Adjectives]

40. J This sentence has no errors, but options F, G, and H are all fragments. [Sentence Recognition]

41. C This sentence has no errors. In option A, the ending quotation mark is misplaced. Option B is missing a comma after *asked,* and *do* should be capitalized. Option D should have no quotation marks because it is not a direct quotation. [Quotation Marks]

42. G The word *north* should not be capitalized unless it refers to a region of the United States. In option F, *city* should be capitalized, while in option H, *Brother* should not be capitalized. In option J, *Surprise Party* should not be capitalized, but *saturday* should be. [Capitalization]

43. C *Work fewer hours and get more done* are parallel—the same structure. Options A, B, and D are not parallel to *work fewer hours*. [Nonparallel Structure]

44. G *These* is plural, to match *skills*, while options F and J are singular. Option H does not make sense. [Reflexive and Demonstrative Pronouns]

45. C *Urgent* and *important* are correct because they are both adjectives, describing *priorities*. Option A has two adverbs, and options B and D each have one adjective and one adverb. [Choosing Between Adjectives and Adverbs]

46. H *Position* ends a question, so it requires a question mark. Option F would be correct if the first sentence were a statement. Option G should have a question mark. Option J is a run-on. [End Marks]

47. B This option contains only one negative (*hardly*), but options A, C, and D each contain two. [Using Negatives]

48. H *Less* should not be used with the *-er* ending or *more* or both, making options F, G, and J incorrect. [Comparative Adverbs]

49. A *Has settled* is correct in the present perfect tense. Option B is not correct because *was* is in the past tense. Option C is not correct because it is in the future perfect tense. The sentence is not correct as it is (option D) because *had* needs to be *has*. [Perfect and Progressive Tenses]

50. F The relative pronoun *who* refers to people. In this case, it refers to *customers*. In options G and J, the relative pronouns refer to things or objects. Option H is not a relative pronoun. [Nominative and Relative Pronouns]

51. D These sentences develop the topic of knowing when to go to the doctor. Options A, B, and C are all slightly off this topic. [Supporting Sentences]

52. G These sentences develop the topic of changing weather patterns. Options F, H, and J are all slightly off this topic. [Supporting Sentences]

53. C *Worse* is an adjective here, comparing a headache at two different times of the day. Options A and B are incorrect forms. Option D should be used to compare more than two things. [Choosing Between Adjectives and Adverbs]

54. G The shop will open in the future. Options F and H are present tense. Option J is past tense. [Present and Future Tenses]

55. A *Who* is a relative pronoun that refers to a person or people. Options B and C are relative pronouns that refer to things or objects. Option D is an object pronoun. [Nominative and Relative Pronouns]

Appendix

Reflexive Pronouns

Singular Form	Plural Form	Examples
myself	ourselves	I quickly made arrangements for *myself*. We should give *ourselves* some credit.
himself, herself, itself	themselves	Frustrated, she decided to do it *herself*. The dog accidentally bit *itself*. The students behaved *themselves*.
yourself	yourselves	You probably should ask him *yourself*. You two should save some cake for *yourselves*.

Demonstrative Pronouns

Singular Form	Plural Form	Examples
this	these	*This* kind of chocolate is my favorite. Please put *these* cookies in a box.
that	those	I have seen *that* man over there before. I remember *those* green eyes.

Perfect Tenses

How to Form Perfect Tenses
have, has, or *had* + verb with *-d* or *-ed* ending.
Present Perfect Used to express action that occurred at an indefinite time in the past. *I have applied there often.*
Past Perfect Used to express an action completed in the past before some other past action or event. *Before I ate breakfast, I had submitted an application.*
Future Perfect Used to show that an action is to be completed before a specific time in the future. *I will have submitted all of my job applications by Friday.*

Progressive Tenses

How to Form the Progressive Tense	
have or *has* + been + verb with *-ing* ending	
Singular	**Plural**
I have been walking.	We have been walking.
You have been walking.	You have been walking.
He/she/it has been walking.	They have been walking.

Examples of Superlative Adjectives

Base Adjective	Number of Syllables	Comparative	Superlative
old	1	older	oldest
large	1	larger	largest
correct	2	more correct	most correct
successful	3	more successful	most successful

Sentence Recognition

How to Recognize a Complete Sentence

- A complete sentence has a subject and a verb and expresses a complete thought.
- It begins with a capital letter and ends with a punctuation mark, such as a period (.), question mark (?), or exclamation point (!).

How to Recognize and Correct a Run-On Sentence

- A run-on sentence is one in which two sentences are written as one.
- A run-on sentence expresses two or more complete thoughts.
- To correct a run-on sentence, use an end punctuation mark to separate the two complete thoughts. Then make the first letter of the second sentence a capital letter.

How to Recognize and Correct a Sentence Fragment

- A sentence that is missing either a subject or a verb—or both—is called a sentence fragment.
- Sentence fragments do not express complete thoughts.
- To correct a sentence fragment, add a subject, a verb, or both to complete the thought.